LIFE AND LETTERS ON THE ROMAN FRONTIER

VINDOLANDA AND ITS PEOPLE

LIFE AND LETTERS ON THE ROMAN FRONTIER

VINDOLANDA AND ITS PEOPLE

ALAN K. BOWMAN

BRITISH MUSEUM PRESS

Published by British Museum Press,
a division of
The British Museum Company Ltd
46 Bloomsbury Street, London WC1B 3QQ

First published 1994
First published in paperback 1998

British Library Cataloguing in Publication Data
A catalogue record for this book is
available from the British Library.

ISBN 0-7141-1389 1 (cased edition)
ISBN 0-7141-23110 (paperback edition)

Designed by Harry Green

Set in Bembo by Rowland Phototypesetting Ltd
Bury St Edmunds, Suffolk
Printed and bound in Great Britain by
The Bath Press

FRONTISPIECE The Roman fort of Vindolanda

CONTENTS

LIST OF ILLUSTRATIONS

ABBREVIATIONS

The standard abbreviations for publications of Greek papyri may be found in E. G. Turner, *Greek papyri, an introduction* (2nd edn, Oxford, 1979) and J. F. Oates, R. S. Bagnall, W. H. Willis, K. A. Worp, *Checklist of editions of Greek papyri and ostraka* (4th edn, Atlanta, 1992). Lists of the conventional citations of the works of classical authors are to be found in: C. T. Lewis, C. Short, *A Latin dictionary* (Oxford, 1879), P. Glare (ed.), *Oxford Latin dictionary* (Oxford, 1968–82), H. G. Liddell, R. Scott, H. S. Jones, *Greek–English lexicon* (9th edn, Oxford, 1940).

AJ	F. F. Abbott, A. C. Johnson, *Municipal administration in the Roman empire*. Princeton, 1926
ANRW	H. Temporini, W. Haase (ed.), *Aufstieg und Niedergang der römischen Welt*. Berlin, 1972–
CEL	P. Cugusi, *Corpus epistularum latinarum papyris, tabulis, ostracis seruatarum*. Florence, 1992
ChLA	A. Bruckner, R. Marichal, *Chartae latinae antiquiores*. Olten/Lausanne, 1954–
CIL	*Corpus inscriptionum latinarum*. Berlin, 1862–
Doc. Masada	H. M. Cotton, J. Geiger, *Masada II, The Yigael Yadin excavations 1963–1965, Final reports, The Latin and Greek documents*. Jerusalem, 1989
EJ	V. Ehrenberg, A. H. M. Jones, *Documents illustrating the reign of Augustus and Tiberius*. 2nd edn, Oxford, 1976
ILS	H. Dessau (ed.), *Inscriptiones latinae selectae*. Berlin, 1892–1916
JEA	*Journal of Egyptian Archaeology*
JRS	*Journal of Roman Studies*
NPEL	A. Mócsy, *Nomenclator prouinciarum Europae latinarum et Galliae Cisalpinae*. Dissertationes Pannonicae III.1. Budapest, 1983
O. Bu Njem	R. Marichal, *Les ostraca de Bu Njem. Libya Antiqua*, Suppl.9. Tripoli, 1992
O. Claud.	J. Bingen *et al.*, *Mons Claudianus, ostraca graeca et latina*. IFAO, Documents de fouilles 29. Cairo, 1992

O. Flor.	R. S. Bagnall, *The Florida ostraca: documents from the Roman army in Upper Egypt*, Greek, Roman and Byzantine Monographs 7. Durham, N. C., 1976
P. Dura	C. B. Welles, R. O. Fink, J. F. Gilliam, *The excavations at Dura-Europus, Final Report V, Part I: the parchments and papyri*. New Haven, 1959
PME	H. Devijver, *Prosopographia militiarum equestrium quae fuerunt ab Augusto ad Gallienum*. Leuven, 1976–87
PNRB	A. L. F. Rivet, C. Smith, *The place-names of Roman Britain*. London, 1979
RIB	R. G. Collingwood, R. P. Wright, *The Roman inscriptions of Britain*. Oxford, 1965–
RMD II	M. M. Roxan, *Roman Military Diplomas 1977–84*. University of London, Institute of Archaeology, Occasional Publication no.9, 1985
RMR	R. O. Fink, *Roman military records on papyrus*. Cleveland, 1971
Tab. Vindol. I	A. K. Bowman, J. D. Thomas, *Vindolanda: the Latin writing-tablets*, Britannia Monograph 4. London, 1983
Tab. Vindol. II	A. K. Bowman, J. D. Thomas, *The Vindolanda writing-tablets (Tabulae Vindolandenses II)*. London, 1994
VRR I	*Vindolanda Research Reports, New Series*, Vol. I, *The early wooden forts. Introduction and analysis of the structures.* Hexham, 1994
VRR II	*Vindolanda Research Reports, New Series*, Vol. II, *Reports on the auxiliaries, the writing tablets, inscriptions, brands and graffiti.* By E. Birley, R. E. Birley, A. R. Birley. Hexham, 1993
VRR III	*Vindolanda Research Reports, New Series*, Vol. III, *Preliminary Reports on the leather, textiles, environmental evidence and dendrochronology.* Hexham, 1993
VRR IV	*Vindolanda Research Reports, New Series*, Vol. IV, *The small finds.* Hexham, 1993
ZPE	*Zeitschrift für Papyrologie und Epigraphik*

1

INTRODUCTION

Despite the very great advances brought by increased archaeological activity in recent years, the poverty of evidence for the period in the history of Roman Britain which lies between the end of Agricola's governorship and the construction of Hadrian's Wall (*c.* AD 85–122) has been striking by comparison with later periods in Britain, and with other provinces of the Roman empire. We have had a skeleton, but a truly fleshless one. Since the resumption of excavations in the early 1970s Vindolanda has established a claim to have given us, in more senses than one, a considerable amount of flesh.

> The archaeologist's spade
> delves into dwellings
> vacancied long ago,
>
> unearthing evidence
> of life-ways no-one
> would dream of leading now,
>
> concerning which he has not much
> to say that he can prove:
> the lucky man!
>
> Knowledge may have its purposes,
> but guessing is always
> much more fun than knowing.

Auden wrote those words in 1973[1] which was, by coincidence, the year in which the most extraordinary product of the excavations at the fort first came to light in the shape of written texts, letters and military documents preserved on wooden tablets.[2]

Precisely what these texts will allow us to prove is perhaps for the reader of the following pages to judge. There is still more than enough room for guesswork.

What is beyond doubt is the fact that a total of more than 250 substantial written texts gives us a very great deal of new evidence. This information has to be teased out of material which is all too often barely legible, fragmentary or obscure (or all three at once). Our ability, such as it is, to read it depends on our predecessors in the field of Latin papyrology and palaeography and, as a token of our debt to an earlier pioneer generation, it is appropriate to identify two of the most distinguished British scholars in these fields by recalling the words of the late Sir Eric Turner in his obituary of Sir Harold Idris Bell, written in 1967: 'I remember Bell's telling me of his hope that one day he would find a letter on papyrus written by a soldier on Roman service in Britain, a hope that has not yet been fulfilled.'[3] Bell would surely have derived pleasure from seeing that hope amply fulfilled in the 1970s and 1980s, even if on wood, rather than papyrus. He would certainly also have derived great pleasure from the fact that my responsibility for editing this material has been shared with the last and most distinguished of his pupils, Professor J. David Thomas of Durham University. That my name alone appears under the title of this publication should not obscure the fact that the credit for any sense which we have been able to extract from these often fragmentary and obscure texts belongs in at least equal measure to him. Our collaboration in this work has extended over two decades.

Like all papyrologists and documentary historians of the ancient world, we live with the awareness that tomorrow's new text may stand today's truth on its head. With writing-tablets still coming out of the ground in the 1990s, it should be obvious that many of our present conclusions can only be tentative and provisional.

There is a great deal to be gained, even so. Our knowledge of roads, forts, archaeological and inscriptional evidence has given us a skeletal history of this period in Britain. Our Vindolanda texts give us, as we shall see, a vast mass of detailed information, but hardly any explicit generalisation of importance. To take two extreme examples, what do we learn of any value from the fact that one of our writers refers in a letter to the possibility of '*tempestates molestae*',[4] that another, writing in the winter months, says that he does not wish to trouble the draft animals *dum viae male* (sc. *malae*) *sunt*?[5] It can hardly be claimed as a major advance that we can recognise the existence of bad roads in winter during Roman times! Our difficulty is to make the detail coherent and coax it to general conclusions that are not merely trite. We have to proceed on the basis that the accretion of detail does actually modify the general picture and change our state of knowledge, surely, if almost imperceptibly; this is advance from within the subject, working within the framework of what we already know, and I hope to be able to show that the significance of this detailed information for northern Britain in the late first and early second centuries AD has some dramatic implications for our general conception of the development of the frontier region and for our knowledge of the character and behaviour of the Roman army as an instrument of imperialism.

It is, nevertheless, appropriate to emphasise what this book is *not*. It is not a history of Roman Britain, nor of the northern frontier, nor the Roman army, nor even of the fort of Vindolanda as a whole in this period. All these topics have been well served by recent research and by publications of scholars far better qualified in those subjects than I am. The general Romano-British context, physical and cultural, is illustrated with a wealth of detail in a recent publication and reports on various aspects of the archaeological excavations of the early wooden forts at Vindolanda have been published.[6] What follows, therefore, is an attempt to describe and analyse specifically what the Vindolanda writing-tablets tell us about various aspects of the early Roman occupation of northern Britain and life in the frontier region, and to say something about the context into which that evidence needs to be put.

This presentation of the evidence of the writing-tablets is, I need hardly say, fundamentally derivative of and secondary to the *editio princeps* of the texts from Vindolanda.[7] The form which the presentation takes in this book, however, is based in large part on the Lees Knowles Lectures in Military History which I gave at Trinity College, Cambridge, in the autumn of 1988. For that opportunity and for their gracious hospitality I am most grateful to the Master and Fellows of Trinity College.

I have gratitude to express on several other counts. To the Vindolanda Trust and particularly to its Director, Robin Birley, who takes the credit for recognising these sodden fragments of wood for what they are, who has continued to conjure them out of the ground over a period of two decades and has constantly encouraged us in our attempts to reveal their secrets. To Dr Ian Longworth and Dr T. W. Potter of the Department of Prehistoric and Romano-British Antiquities at the British Museum, where the tablets have now come to rest. To Alison Rutherford, formerly of the University of Newcastle upon Tyne, to Eric Hitchcock, formerly of University College, London and to David Webb of the British Museum Photographic Service, for achieving photographic miracles without which we would hardly have been able to contemplate reading anything at all. On matters papyrological and Romano-British I have been helped by a very large number of scholars who have made helpful comments either in writing or in person. They will, I hope, understand that it is impossible to acknowledge each individual debt. To J. N. Adams, S. S. Frere, M. W. C. Hassall, G. D. B. Jones, J. R. Rea, R. S. O. Tomlin, J.-P. Wild, J. J. Wilkes special thanks are due for making this work less imperfect than it would otherwise have been. Neither they nor my many unnamed creditors are responsible for the remaining errors or follies. I am grateful to Dr N. P. Milner for valuable bibliographical assistance.

Publication of the writing-tablets from Vindolanda over the past two decades has been generously supported by the Trustees of the Haverfield Bequest and by Mr H. A. Orr-Ewing. The Governing Body of Christ Church, Oxford, has been generous in helping to provide resources and time needed for research. In 1991–3 I was awarded the British Academy (Marc Fitch) Readership in the Humanities in order to enable me to complete my share of the work on this project. I am most grateful for the very necessary freedom from other commitments which this Readership has provided.

Addendum Four further seasons of excavation took place at Vindolanda in 1991–4, yielding about 400 new ink tablets and several dozen stilus tablets. It is estimated that there are between seventy and eighty substantial new ink texts which Professor Thomas and I intend to publish in the near future. A handful of these texts have received preliminary publication[8] and I have taken the opportunity to add the most interesting of these to Appendix II. I have also been able to make some minor corrections and to add a few essential items to the bibliography. [September, 1997]

NOTES

1 'Archaeology', W. H. Auden, *Collected Poems* (London, 1976), 662.

2 See R. E. Birley (1977), 132–4, Bowman and Thomas (1983), 19–24.

3 *JRS* 57 (1967), xiii.

4 **17**.ii.6–8 (see note 7, below).

5 **32**.ii.20–1 (see note 7, below).

6 Jones and Mattingly (1990), *VRR* I–V.

7 *Tab. Vindol.* II. References in boldface are to the texts as numbered in Appendix II of the present book. Other texts are referred to by the publication numbers assigned *Tab. Vindol.* II. These are numbered in a continuous series but note that *Tab. Vindol.* II contains re-editions, with new numbers, of the texts first edited in *Tab. Vindol.* I.

8 See Birley and Birley (1994), Bowman and Thomas (1996). For comparable and interesting new material from Carlisle see now Tomlin (1998).

2

THE WRITING-TABLETS

The preservation, recognition and recovery of large quantities of written material at a key site in the development of the northern frontier of the Roman empire in the period before the construction of Hadrian's Wall is one of the most important and exciting recent developments in Romano-British archaeology and history. The writing-tablets afford a uniquely detailed view of aspects of the Roman occupation of Britain for which there has hitherto been scarcely any evidence at all. Historians have had largely to base their reconstructions of this period in the history of Roman Britain on one historical account, the *Agricola* of Tacitus, a number of inscriptions, the evidence of archaeological sites and a large quantity of artefacts.[1] Whilst this body of evidence is by no means negligible, it does contain immense gaps. The Vindolanda writing-tablets add an enormous and invaluable amount of depth and detail – evidence of this kind and on this scale is quite simply unparalleled.

As for the context in which these documents must be placed, the archaeology at Vindolanda has its own story to tell and it can be reviewed only very briefly here. Robin Birley's analysis shows that in the early forts at Vindolanda which have given us the writing-tablets five periods of occupation can be identified; the dates assigned to these periods have to be treated with the caution which must always be applied to such indications. The earliest fort begins *c.* AD 85 and terminates *c.* AD 92 (Period 1); the fort is then enlarged and Periods 2 and 3 run down to *c.* AD 103 (Period 2 *c.* AD 92–7, Period 3 *c.* AD 97–102/3); after a short hiatus, Period 4 perhaps begins in AD 104 and takes us to about AD 120, and the occupation of Period 5 lies between the years AD 120 and 130.[2] The period shortly after AD 90, from which the earliest of the writing-tablets appear to derive, may be crucial in the establishment of the pre-Hadrianic, Stanegate frontier (fig. 1). The enlargement of the fort at Vindolanda probably fits into a pattern which is repeated elsewhere at important sites in the frontier region and it suggests that this phase of construction was the central feature of a new phase of Roman policy. This will have been initiated shortly after the decision was taken, late in the 80s, to abandon the greater part of the territory in Scotland which Agricola's last campaigns covered.[3] The three decades between AD 90 and 120, immediately prior to the commencement of Hadrian's Wall, mark an important phase in the history of the frontier and it is precisely this period which the Vindolanda writing-tablets illuminate.

The excavations have examined the southern part of the central range on and adjacent to the *via principalis* of the enlarged fort. Writing-tablets have been found certainly located in contexts which associate them with Periods 2, 3, 4 and 5, from *c.* AD 92 onwards. The handful of tablets which were found in the ditch on the west side of the Period 1 fort are more likely to be part of the debris from Period 2. The great majority of the tablets cluster in Periods 2 and 3, both on the street and in the adjacent buildings. Of these, the most important are the timber buildings which fronted the street on the east side. These buildings certainly formed part of the *praetorium*, the residence of the commanding officers of units stationed at Vindolanda during Periods 2 and 3, the latter phase a rebuilding of a substantially higher quality than the former. The main living quarters of the officers and their families probably lay beneath the later stone fort and are now inaccessible. The rooms on the west side, which have been excavated, seem to include a large yard, a kitchen and storeroom and may have been devoted to the domestic services and organisation. The scatter of tablets in these rooms and on the street, where some attempt (fortunately not entirely successful) was made to burn them, perhaps suggests that they were carried out as rubbish from the inner rooms and taken to bonfires on the street when the building was abandoned or rebuilt, and remains of the bonfire of tablets have now been discovered.[4]

During Period 4, from which we have a smaller number of tablets, but some very important items, the area of the earlier *praetorium* seems to have been occupied by a barrack-block, the southern end of which was sealed off from the rest, perhaps to form the living quarters of the centurions or *optiones*. The function of the building from Period 5 is more problematic, but it seems likely to have been a workshop (*fabrica*).[5]

The tablets were deposited in layers of bracken and straw flooring in successive occupation levels in the buildings and on the street outside. These deposits, some of which show signs of incineration, look like the result of dumping of rubbish and contain a wide variety of other organic remains and artefacts. The location of the early finds suggested that the presence of organic remains, in particular human urine and excreta, might have been significant in creating chemical conditions crucial for the preservation of the wooden tablets. As the excavations progressed, however, tablets were found in areas where these conditions did not obtain and it now seems likely that the damp, anaerobic environment is sufficient to account for the preservation.[6]

The quantity of material is, by the standards of the survival of evidence at ancient sites, very considerable. Almost 50 substantial texts were published in 1983 from well over 1000 fragments. The continuous series of inventory numbers of tablets found in 1985–9 runs to just under 1000 and has yielded well over 200 further texts of significance. The investigation is proceeding northwards along the line of the *via principalis* and tablets are continuing to emerge, although not on the scale of previous finds.

When the first of the Vindolanda writing-tablets was discovered in 1973, the feature which aroused a great deal of surprise and interest – and still seems no less remarkable – was the type of writing-material used. We have been accustomed to expect Roman wooden tablets to be of the familiar stilus type, hollowed out in the centre, filled with wax and incised with a metal stilus which may or may not leave traces of the writing on the wood when the wax has perished. The excavations at Vindolanda have, indeed, produced over 100 tablets of this type (including fragments, as well as several which seem to have be re-used),[7] but the vast majority are quite different. They are thin leaves of wood, normally between 1 and 3mm thick and about the size of a modern postcard, with a reasonably smooth surface intended to take writing in ink. Texts of this kind on papyrus were normally written with a reed pen and this certainly seems to have been the practice at Vindolanda also.[8] It is clear that the ink was the normal mixture of carbon, gum arabic and water. In many cases the tablets were folded, after the text was written, in such a way that the writing was on the inner faces and was thus protected; one result of this practice is that wet ink sometimes produces offsets on the facing surfaces (pl. VIII).

These leaf tablets, as we have called them, were cut from wood rather than bark and were clearly the counterpart of papyrus in those areas of the empire where papyrus will have been difficult and expensive to obtain. They were presumably cheap and easy to make, especially in places where military technology was readily available. We do not know precisely how they were cut, but it is perhaps relevant that we have abundant evidence in artefacts and in literary sources for the manufacture of fine furniture veneers.[9] Despite their almost complete absence from the archaeological record before the discoveries at

Vindolanda, we can find evidence that such tablets were perfectly well-known in the Roman world.[10] The historian Herodian, writing in the third century AD about the death of the emperor Commodus (AD 180–92), noted that the assassination was occasioned by the discovery that he had made a list of proscribed persons 'taking a writing-tablet of the kind that were made from lime-wood, cut into thin sheets and folded face-to-face by being bent'.[11] Cassius Dio, writing at the beginning of the third century, also mentions 'tablets of the sort which are made from lime-wood' in a story about Ulpius Marcellus, governor of Britain in the reign of Commodus.[12] Marcellus is said to have used them while on campaign in the north and this presupposes their presence in the frontier area – a detail which the Vindolanda finds most strikingly confirm. The Vindolanda examples are, of course, not made from lime which was not native to this area. Botanical analysis has revealed the use of birch, alder and oak, all of which grew locally. By contrast, the stilus tablets were clearly made from non-native wood and imported as manufactured objects.

The fact that Vindolanda is unique in having yielded such a large number of leaf tablets of such high quality should not lead to the inference that such material was not present at other sites. Discoveries in the last two decades, at Caerleon and Carlisle for example, assure us that, even if large quantities of tablets were not deposited in such concentration, they were nevertheless in everyday use and circulation.[13] This alone is an advance in knowledge which will necessitate a radical revision of the history of writing and writing-materials in classical antiquity.

The deposit at Vindolanda contains a mixture of letters and documents, personal and administrative, which were thrown out as the area in the central southern sector of the enlarged fort was rebuilt or re-occupied in successive phases. It is important to emphasise that this cannot have been the location of the official record-office of the fort, which will have been situated within the headquarters building (*principia*) in the central sector of the site. It is perhaps unlikely that the contents of the record-office will have been thrown out in this manner when the unit or units in garrison moved on – they are more likely to have been destroyed or moved with the unit which generated them. Documents from a military record-office have been discovered at Bu Njem in Libya and we no doubt owe the preservation of papyri from the archives of the Twentieth Cohort of Palmyrene Archers, stationed at Doura-Europos on the Euphrates in the mid-third century AD, to the fact that the fort was captured by the Persians in the 250s.[14] At Vindolanda we have a sample of the written material which ended up in the commanding officers' residence or was generated there, or in the later barrack-block and workshop – in many ways an even more interesting and varied mixture. The range of subject-matter and content is truly astonishing, especially in the context of the frontier area of a province which had no previous history of urban or literate culture.

The military documents include important texts relating to the strength and the activities of the units stationed at Vindolanda in the period between AD 90 and 120, as well as routine reports.[15] These may well have been copies of documents which were deposited in the official archives or interim reports sent to the commanding officer. The same may be true of some of the accounts which clearly relate to the military administration.[16] Many of the other accounts, however, seem more likely to relate to the domestic administration of the *praetorium* itself.[17] It seems safe to assume that these documents and accounts were generated at Vindolanda. The situation as regards the correspondence – by far the largest category – is rather more complicated. First of all, we have a number of groups of letters associated with particular individuals. The most extensive is the correspondence of Flavius Cerialis, prefect of the Ninth Cohort of Batavians, and there is a small group associated with his wife Sulpicia Lepidina.[18] We have been able to assign more than sixty texts to the correspondence of Cerialis. This belongs in Period 3 and it may well be that much if not most of the material from this period, which provides by far the largest proportion of our writing-tablets, relates to Cerialis and his time at Vindolanda. Smaller groups of tablets belong to individual officers named Julius Verecundus, Flavius Genialis and Priscinus and others to a decurion named Lucius and to a certain Cassius Saecularis, perhaps a centurion or an *optio*.[19] Of the officers, Verecundus and Genialis seem to have been at Vindolanda in the earlier part of the period covered by the writing-tablets and Priscinus somewhat later.

The chronological indications offered by the archaeological data allow us to place Flavius Cerialis and his family in Period 3 (*c.* AD 97–102/3) with confidence. In all the other groups of tablets (as indeed in that of Cerialis too) there is some variation in the periods to which particular tablets are attributed and dates assigned to them must be treated with caution. Some individuals might, of course, have been at Vindolanda for long periods of time or on more than one posting but it is also a fact of archaeological life that objects are found in chronological contexts to which they ought not to belong. Whilst there is no objection to using the archaeological context as a general chronological indicator, it is better to avoid basing any detailed argument or reconstructed sequence of occupation on the periods to which the various tablets are attributed.[20]

We might expect that much of this and the other correspondence must have originated elsewhere – at other sites in Britain and perhaps also in Gaul. Not all came from elsewhere, however, for we have drafts or file copies of letters written by people at Vindolanda (including Cerialis), and letters received by people elsewhere and brought with them to Vindolanda where they were deposited; we perhaps also ought to envisage the possibility of letters exchanged by people serving in different units brigaded together at Vindolanda.[21] The content of the letters is varied. Some are strictly personal and social, others refer to military matters such as the despatch of soldiers or items of equipment, yet others are a mixture.

If this is much as one might expect, it is perhaps worth emphasising yet again Vindolanda's capacity to surprise us. We have at least one tablet which certainly contains a literary text, a line of Virgil's *Aeneid*, and there are three others which might be literary or semi-literary in character.[22] A handful of tablets provide the only known examples of Latin shorthand from classical antiquity.[23] These alone strikingly illustrate some of the respects in which the pre-Hadrianic fort at Vindolanda provides by far the most important body of evidence for the use of writing-materials and the development of Latin handwriting in the early Roman empire.

How much of a cross-section of the whole community at Vindolanda (and elsewhere) all this material represents is a matter of some interest and is discussed in more detail below. There can be no doubt that it gives us a very immediate access to a large number of the people on the northern frontier in a coherent area and period. It yields us a vivid and detailed series of snapshots of the lifestyle of the occupying forces and their impact on the environment. With the evidence of the Vindolanda tablets, we are truly at the heart of the romanisation of the province of Britannia.

NOTES

1 The best recent, general account is to be found in Frere (1987), chs 6 and 7.
2 *VRR* I.
3 For this important hypothesis see Jones (1990).
4 R. E. Birley (pers. comm., September, 1993).
5 *VRR* I. It is worth noting that the distinction between barrack-block and workshop is not always clear-cut and that a barrack-block might contain a workshop area; see Glasbergen and Groenman-van Waateringe (1974), 11, 25.
6 *Tab. Vindol.* I, pp. 22–4, *VRR* III, 116.

7 *Tab. Vindol.* I 107–17, cf. pp. 44–5. Most of the stilus tablets come from the excavations of the 1980s and the texts are generally very difficult to read. The addresses are usually the most legible parts; for some examples see *Tab. Vindol.* II, p. 364.

8 See R. E. Birley (1990), 6, *VRR* II, 16. Note the view that objects formerly identified as 'ox-goads' are in fact pens with iron coiled nibs.

9 Pliny, *Natural History*, 16.68, cf. *Tab. Vindol.* I, pp. 29–30.

10 It is perhaps tablets of this kind which are denoted by the word *pugillar*, indicating that they are 'fist-sized', which occurs frequently in the contemporary authors Juvenal and Martial and occasionally in documents (e.g. *ChLA* V 301, *pugillaribus codicibus*). It is interesting that this Latin word eventually passed into Welsh as *peuwllawr*. Cf. Stevenson (1990), 20–1.

11 Herodian, 1.17.1.

12 Cassius Dio 72.8.2.

13 See Tomlin (1986) and (1992).

14 *O. Bu Njem*, pp. 5–10, *P. Dura*, pp. 3–4, 36.

15 **1**, **2**, **4**, *Tab. Vindol.* II 127–60.

16 E.g. **6**, *Tab. Vindol.* II 178.

17 E.g. **10**, **11**, **13**, **14**.

18 Cerialis, *Tab. Vindol.* II 225–90; Lepidina, *Tab. Vindol.* II 291–4.

19 Verecundus, *Tab. Vindol.* II 210–12; Genialis, *Tab. Vindol.* II 217–24; Priscinus, *Tab. Vindol.* II 295–8; Lucius, *Tab. Vindol.* II 299–300; Cassius Saecularis, *Tab. Vindol.* II 213–16.

20 For a more strictly chronological treatment see *VRR* II, 18–72.

21 Draft, **15**; file copy, **16**; letters brought from elsewhere, **28**, **30**, cf. *Tab. Vindol.* II, pp. 43–5; internal correspondence, perhaps *Tab. Vindol.* II 328.

22 *Tab. Vindol.* II, 118–21.

23 *Tab. Vindol.* II 122–6, cf. Teitler (1985), 44–9, Ganz (1990).

3

STRATEGIES OF OCCUPATION

Military matters are central to our interpretation of the early stages of the Roman occupation of the province of Britannia. The steady accretion of archaeological and inscriptional evidence has taken us well beyond the basic historical framework defined by well-known events, the invasion by the emperor Claudius, the revolt of Boudica and the Iceni in the reign of Nero, the seven campaigning seasons of Agricola which took the Roman presence by the mid-80s to the north of Scotland, the building of Hadrian's Wall.[1] It is not difficult to see how historians and archaeologists of the current generation have extended the horizons of the subject. The library shelves are replete with volumes attesting increasing interest in the development of trade and urbanisation, the interaction between town and countryside, the construction of models which illuminate the relationship between the core of the empire and its periphery.[2] Even the most superficial perusal of these volumes will soon reveal, however, that the surface of these topics hardly needs a scratch before the importance of the Roman military presence becomes as apparent and pervasive as King Charles's head in the imagination of the unfortunate Mr Dick. Not all that surprising, one might think, since despite our predilection for social and economic history, the overwhelming majority of our evidence for the first century of Roman rule in Britain, archaeological and inscriptional, is generated by the activities, the needs and the influence of the Roman army.

It goes without saying that conquest and subjugation were more than a matter of fighting battles and establishing garrisons. The character and presence of the army are central to everything implied by the concept of romanisation. In the north of England, the period between the departure of Agricola and the completion of Hadrian's Wall (c. AD 85–late 120s) was crucial. After Agricola a sober policy prescribed retrenchment rather than expansion. *Perdomita Britannia et statim omissa* ('Britain was subjugated and immediately let slip'), complained Tacitus, but he was not an impartial commentator for that policy was that of the hated and tyrannical emperor Domitian and the conquering governor was Agricola, the father of Tacitus' wife.[3] The completion of Hadrian's Wall some 40 years later is habitually, but perhaps a trifle misleadingly, regarded as the most emphatic symbol of the limits of Roman *imperium* in the island. If it was so regarded by Hadrian, his successor evidently did not view it as a permanently preclusive frontier. Renewed occupation of military posts to the north and, in due course, the construction of the Antonine Wall are emphatic signs of Roman interest in the area to the north of Hadrian's Wall.

The years between AD 80 and 120 are rightly regarded as the period when the northern frontier of Britain was established and its region organised (see fig. 1). Our understanding of the history of the Vindolanda site as a whole is crucial to the interpretation of this development. Before the building of Hadrian's Wall, the main line of the frontier system was the so-called Stanegate, on which the early forts at Vindolanda occupy a crucial position, along with Carlisle and Corbridge (which show signs of their military importance as early as the 70s). The Roman hold on Scotland established under Agricola was relinquished in AD 87 and it has recently been suggested that the strategic emphasis of the post-Agricolan arrangement lay on the Tyne–Solway axis itself, garrisoned by a number of large forts which were expanded *c.* AD 90 – Carlisle, Vindolanda and Corbridge and perhaps also Burgh-by-Sands, Nether Denton, Carvoran and Newbrough, a series of forts linked by a system of roads and ditches. Some modification may have taken place *c.* AD 103 and a new phase of development of fortlets between the major sites may have been initiated.[4] Be that as it may, the broader picture of development in the frontier zone demands that we pay attention not merely to the defence of a line, but also to the details of the military, economic and social articulation of the frontier zone, supported by an established infrastructure of forts and roads in Brigantia (that is, North Yorkshire, the Pennines, and Cumbria).[5]

How was the frontier organised and garrisoned? A road, a fort, a military unit can be placed on the map or identified in an inscription. An outline of the 'grand strategy' emphasises a move in the Flavian period to more clearly defined frontier lines, with permanent forts and garrisons, linked by communication systems which enabled the army to mass in the face of a coherent military threat; in peacetime the forts functioned as nodal points in the communication system, enabling areas to be, in effect, cordoned off and controlled. In Britain, the frontier region was manned by auxiliary units, with the legions stationed at crucial strategic points to the rear, at York, Chester and Caerleon.

In considering the picture as it emerges at Vindolanda we should begin with a single text – perhaps the most important military document ever found in Britain, written on an extraordinarily large diptych.[6] For our general conception of military organisation, this text is uniquely illuminating. It was found in the ditch at the west side of the Period 1 fort, but is more likely to relate to the occupation in Period 2 (*c.* AD 92–7). It contains a strength report of the First Cohort of Tungrians which must have formed part of the garrison at Vindolanda when the report was written. The cohort is also mentioned in one of the letters from Vindolanda. It was previously known in its fully developed form as a milliary infantry unit stationed in northern Britain in this period and is attested in the second and third centuries at Carrawburgh, Castlecary and Housesteads on Hadrian's Wall.[7] Its strength report roughly follows the form we would expect from parallels in papyri from Egypt. But it is worth emphasising that this is the only known strength report from Britain and the only example for a milliary cohort of auxiliary troops. It gives first a heading with standard elements: the month and day, but not the year (18 May); then the statement that this is the net strength (*n(umerus) p(urus)*) of the First Cohort of Tungrians whose commander is Julius Verecundus; then the total strength of 752 men, including 6 centurions. Then follows the breakdown, beginning with the list of those absent: there are 46 *singulares legati*, troops detached for service as guards with the governor of the province and assigned on this occasion to the office of a certain Ferox, who might well have been a legionary legate, perhaps in command of the Ninth Legion (Hispana) at York. Then there are detachments at seven different places or on different tours of duty, the details of which are not now legible: the first is at a place named Coria, which probably has 337 including one or two centurions, the second is probably a single centurion, at London. Then the total number of *absentes* is given as 456 including 5 centurions. Then follows the balance of those present (*reliqui praesentes*), 296 including one centurion. This is further broken down: there are 31 unfit for service comprising 15 sick (*aegri*), 6 wounded (*volnerati*) and 10 suffering from inflammation of the eyes (*lippientes*), leaving 265 fit for active service (*valentes*).

This text gives us a great deal of important detail. Not least, we can now be confident that the place called Coria (the name occurs on two or three other occasions in the tablets) must be Corbridge and put an end to a long-running debate about its Latin name. The total size of the unit, 752 men, is close enough to the complement of 800 which is thought to be, in practice, the normal strength of a milliary unit, but the Tungrian cohort is unusual in that it has only 6 centurions, compared with the complement of 10 which was normal for a milliary unit. It may be that we are here looking at a unit which started life as a quingenary cohort in the middle of the process of enlargement and reorganisation.[8]

The general significance of the report for our appreciation of the Roman frontier strategy cannot be overemphasised. Two thirds of the unit are absent from the home base, one centurion as far afield as London, with the largest section nearby at Corbridge which must have had its own home-based unit too. Unfortunately, the whereabouts and activities of detached groups of 6, 9, 11 and 45 men are not legible; for the latter, at least, one possiblity for a detachment of this size is that it was in garrison at an outpost or fortlet in the region. The small number of wounded suggests that this is not an abnormal wartime situation. We can thus begin to revise our whole understanding of the basis of the organisation of forts and garrisons by questioning the notion that forts were built for and garrisoned by individual units of a specific size and type. There was evidently a great deal of movement, splitting of units, brigading of parts of different units together and, as we shall see, maintenance of close communication between forts and personnel. This is a scenario which accommodates much of our other evidence better than more rigid notions of a frontier garrison with a fixed deployment. It fits perfectly, for example, with the evidence for the Flavian period fort at Strageath, where analysis of the buildings has prompted the speculation that the garrison will have consisted at first of a 500-strong part-mounted cohort minus one century and 2 *turmae*, 4 *turmae* and 3 (under-strength) centuries of another part-mounted cohort and a legionary century; and, under revised arrangements, a part-mounted cohort with 4 *turmae* but missing 2 of its 6 centuries and 4 *turmae* and 3 centuries of a second cohort; the area of 4.36 acres could have held a milliary garrison. Similarly, two auxiliary units were brigaded together at Dalswinton. It is perhaps not surprising, therefore, that archaeologists have encountered serious difficulties in attempting to link the evidence for the physical layout of auxiliary forts with the type and organisation of the units which are known or supposed to have garrisoned them.[9] It is worth observing that if the Tungrian strength report does belong to the fort of Period 1, this portion of the cohort might have represented the total garrison force; but if, as is more likely, it relates to the enlarged fort of Period 2, a maximum area of 7 acres, there might well have been other units or part-units, probably of Batavians, present at the same time.

Detailed re-interpretation of the nature and development of the Roman frontier strategy in this region is now under way and the evidence from

Vindolanda – both archaeological and written – is the keystone. The phase of development which culminated in the 120s in the move from the Stanegate frontier to Hadrian's Wall may begin *c.* AD 90.[10] The individual dispositions invite comparison with some of the characteristics of the organisation of frontier armies in the later period when units were reduced in size and deployed in a larger number of positions. Whatever other important changes we may see in the later Roman frontier strategy, this aspect may, then, be more of a formalisation than a real change. Second, the degree of movement and fluidity which the Tungrian strength report illustrates has several advantages, not the least being that it might reduce the possibility of coherent units with common interests or background threatening revolt or insubordination – a sign of lessons learned from the Pannonian revolt (AD 6–9), the mutiny of the Rhine legions (AD 14) and the revolt of Florus and Savrovir in Gallia Belgica (AD 21).[11] Third, the extended military coverage of the frontier zone is achieved not just by means of lightly manned guard-posts but more substantial sections of cohorts and cavalry units (*alae*) as well; this will surely imply the occupation of a greater number of posts in this area than we actually know; our Tungrian strength report may list detached groups at three such posts since and there are several other unidentifiable place-names elsewhere in our tablets which may conceal such stations.[12]

This means that the spread is rather thinner, the communications more embracing and coherent, and the psychology is completely different from something based on the relatively rare need to confront in battle. The frontier line is not so much a system of continuous perimeter defence, nor even a symbolic division between Roman and non-Roman, but the basis of a continuous and active process of policing, organisation and control involving intensive exchange of information in the frontier zone itself and in the regional infrastructure to the rear.[13] It is on this basis that we might perhaps begin to answer the question how is the Roman occupation made effective with so few troops? The military presence can be made to seem stronger and more pervasive than it actually is, numerically, to the scattered and less organised tribal units which might not perceive that forts were not always fully manned. Scattered detachments of Roman troops could coagulate relatively swiftly to exhibit strength in numbers. One feature which, on reflection, is absolutely central to the effectiveness of such an operation is precisely that which Vindolanda above all reveals – the extent and coherence of written communication. Without such communication the native Britons would conspicuously lack the ability to assess the strength and coherence of the opposition.

Around AD 92, the fort at Vindolanda was rebuilt and doubled in size, perhaps as part of a more general pattern of development in the frontier region which has been characterised as a long prelude to the construction of Hadrian's Wall. In Periods 2 and 3, where the majority of our texts lie, we have clear evidence for the presence of the Ninth Cohort of Batavians, probably a 500-strong cohort. We do not know whether it was a part-mounted unit (*cohors equitata*) but there is some evidence for the presence of cavalry at Vindolanda.[14] Some of the officers whose names occur in the tablets may well have commanded the Batavian cohort but the only one of whom we can be certain is Flavius Cerialis who was prefect of the cohort in the period around AD 100. Cerialis, like other officers, is identifiable in several of the addresses written on the backs of the letters which give the name, and sometimes the rank and unit of the addressee. He is by far the best represented figure in the tablets and a substantial portion of the tablets from Period 3 may belong to his papers.[15] Two other texts mention the Third Cohort of Batavians, though not the name of its prefect, and it is possible that this unit too, or parts of it, was at Vindolanda during the period *c.* AD 92–102/3. One letter is addressed to someone connected with the Third Cohort and in another letter to Flavius Cerialis, prefect of the Ninth Cohort, the writer, a decurion named Vitalis, mentions that he (Cerialis) has received letters brought by a centurion of the Third Cohort. This suggests the possibility that the two units, or parts of them, were at Vindolanda at the same time. Their presence in Britain at this period is not otherwise known. Around 103, or shortly thereafter, both these units were moved to the Danube region, where they are attested on inscriptions, perhaps as part of the build-up to Trajan's Second Dacian War (AD 105–6).[16]

About Period 4, which may begin *c.* AD 104 and go on until *c.* AD 120, we are a little more in the dark. If it ever left Vindolanda, the Tungrian unit seems to have reappeared there, perhaps reduced in size, for we know that at some point between AD 103 and 122 it was reduced to quingenary size for a few years. It is entirely possible that some part of it may have maintained its presence at Vindolanda into the period of the building of Hadrian's Wall. A letter attributed to Period 4 to one Priscinus refers to his having despatched soldiers of the First Tungrian cohort from Vindolanda to the governor via Ribchester (Bremetennacum) and one of the accounts from this period includes the name of a certain Sabinus who is described as being from Trier (*Trever*), an origin which would certainly fit with membership of a Tungrian unit. Equally suggestive is the fact that a diploma of AD 146 discovered at Vindolanda was issued to a veteran of the

First Tungrian Cohort who will have joined the unit in AD 121. But another letter, addressed to a decurion, implies the presence of cavalry which the Tungrian unit did not possess. So, there must have been another unit, or part of one, in the garrison as well. We could perhaps make a connection with an entry in an account from this period which names the *equites Vardulli*, a cavalry detachment, presumably from the Spanish First Cohort of Vardulli, known to have been in the region at this time. An equally interesting piece of information emerges from an account of this period which includes a reference to '*militibus legionaribus*' [*sic*]; there has been hitherto no sign of the presence of legionaries at Vindolanda, though their activity in Wall-building after AD 122 is, of course, clear. Now we may have some antecedent evidence, perhaps from the period immediately before the commencement of Hadrian's Wall.[17]

The Batavian units and the Tungrian cohort, which were clearly the main elements in the Vindolanda garrison during the pre-Hadrianic period, will repay a little more attention in the context of the first phase of the occupation of Brigantia and northern Britain. We know that units raised in these areas of Gallia Belgica were closely connected and that four Batavian and two Tungrian units fought under Agricola at the battle of Mons Graupius. It would be extremely surprising if our three Vindolanda units were not among these six. The Batavians, from the region around the mouth of the Rhine/Scheldt, had long enjoyed a special relationship with Rome. Batavian troops were renowned for their horsemanship and had been heavily used in Britain in the conquest period. There can be no doubt that the Batavian revolt of AD 69/70 seriously disrupted the region until it was eventually suppressed by the Roman general Petillius Cerialis, later to govern Britain and to begin the conquest of Brigantia. Whether or not the pre-existing units were cashiered and replaced by new enrollments among loyal elements in the region, however, it is evident that Batavian units continued to form an important part of the army of the north-western empire, and were soon to find their way to Britain. Petillius Cerialis might well have played a central role in their recruitment and transfer. One significant feature of Batavian units was that Rome had traditionally allowed them to be commanded by their own nobles and there is no reason to believe this practice was abandoned in the wake of the revolt. Indeed, we know of at least one Batavian noble in command of a cavalry unit, one Claudius Labeo, who was loyal to Rome throughout the revolt.[18] The existence of such native commanders evokes interesting comparisons, with Arminius the German, for example, or the Pannonians, or the Belgic Gauls of the time of Florus and Sacrovir; however, local loyalties were less dangerous when the unit was not allowed to serve in its native region.[19]

The peculiar relationship between Rome and the Batavians invites us to focus attention briefly on a central figure in our tablets – the *praefectus* of the Ninth Cohort of Batavians, Flavius Cerialis. His possession of the family name of the ruling dynasty, Flavius, strongly implies that the Roman citizenship was acquired by Cerialis or an ancestor not earlier than AD 70 and the *cognomen* may suggest a connection with Petillius Cerialis, perhaps forged in the context of loyalty to Rome during the revolt of AD 69/70. The father of our prefect, then, might be the first Roman citizen of his family. Alternatively, and just conceivably, it might be the prefect himself who was perhaps enfranchised in AD 70 at the age of about 20 and rose to equestrian status and the command of a cohort some 30 years later. The name of Flavius Cerialis' wife tempts us to one further hypothesis; her origin is unknown but Sulpicia Lepidina might be a member of a family first granted citizenship in the short reign of the emperor Ser. Sulpicius Galba (AD 68–9).

The Tungrians originate a little further to the south, in the region of the middle Meuse, and their links with Batavians are emphasised by the diploma of one C. Petillius Vindex (the name, again, evokes a connection with Petillius Cerialis), a Batavian who served in a Tungrian unit in Britain and returned home after service. The establishment and use of these Tungrian and Batavian units in Britain is predicated upon the earlier stages of romanisation in northern Gaul – the process is indicated by the fact that a *civitas Batavorum* – is recorded in an inscription from Holland from the first half of the first century AD.[20] What is interesting about this is the way in which it shows how areas of the periphery of the empire were controlled and organised through the medium of troops from an area which was itself peripheral until relatively recently; if we are correct about the origins of Cerialis, this will apply to some extent to the officer class as well. So the main instrument of domination and romanisation included units and officers whose origins were not at the romanised centre of the empire (Italy, Spain, southern Gaul) but in regions that were still only tenuously controlled at the end of the Julio-Claudian period, a mere 30 years before the appearance of Cerialis and his cohort at Vindolanda.

Our appreciation of the strategy of control will be amplified by a more detailed consideration of the activities and interaction of the military elements in this region (below). Here we may note some further items of evidence in our Vindolanda tablets which suggest features of broader importance. First, there is a tantalising fragment containing a clear reference to the administration of the census. There is evidence for a census officer at Colchester in the early years of the second century and for a *censitor Brittonum Anavio(nensium)* in northern Britain (though the precise location is unknown) towards the end of Trajan's reign. The census is crucial to the organisation of newly acquired regions, and as a potent symbol of subjection to Rome, implying the imposition of taxation, it had been a frequent cause of resentment, in Judaea, Gaul, Germany. This is likely to have been its first incidence in this region of Britain and it will surely have been organised by and through the military officers as part and parcel of the settlement of the frontier zone. No doubt the equestrian officers, like Flavius Cerialis, in charge of units, will have played an important role, as they are known to have done elsewhere, but the key figures in the local organisation may have been the centurions who moved around individually, or in charge of detachments, sometimes carrying correspondence, in the local region and as far afield as London, as the strength report of the Tungrian cohort shows.[21]

Second, there is a letter to the prefect Cerialis from a certain Karus, in all likelihood one Claudius Karus who occurs in another fragment and is probably a fellow-officer. It is a letter of recommendation (*litterae commendaticiae*), a well-known genre, in which Karus invites Cerialis, in terms comparable with those used for such purposes by Cicero and the younger Pliny, to offer patronage to a certain Brigionus and, in turn, to pass Brigionus on to the notice of a more powerful figure, Annius Equester, the legionary *centurio regionarius* at Luguvalium (Carlisle). Equester may well be the most powerful officer in the immediate region; Carlisle is clearly strategically central and this is the earliest attestation of a *centurio regionarius* in Britain or elsewhere. If we were to guess who might be responsible for the organisation of the census in this region, such an officer, with his headquarters at Luguvalium, would come high on the list of possibilities. As for Brigionus, he is evidently of fairly humble station, perhaps not even necessarily a soldier. The name is palpably Gallic or Celtic, given a Latin termination; he might be a native Briton, but certainty on this point eludes us. If he were, we would be glimpsing one of the mechanisms by which the subjects of the frontier region were absorbed into the system.[22]

In fact, our texts give us virtually no evidence at all for the acculturation of the natives. They are mentioned collectively in only one text, a fascinating but enigmatic piece, which is hard to classify. Its brief message shows a clear interest in the fighting characteristics of the natives, probably referring to their lack of armour, the presence of cavalry and the fact that they do not use swords or throw javelins from horseback. We can only guess at the purpose of the text. Perhaps it is a memorandum left for a newly appointed prefect by his predecessor or the commander of a neighbouring fort to acquaint him with the local context – Batavians might be particularly well fitted to combat native cavalry; possibly it is directed to Cerialis who might have arrived at Vindolanda only recently. A commander of an *ala* in fourth-century Egypt was advised to leave instructions for his predecessor: *de singulis etiam pro tutela publica observandis instruere [cura] ne quam sub primitiis saltem suis erroris titubantiam incurat* ('take care to instruct him in all the rules to be followed to guarantee public safety, in order to safeguard him from liabilities and mistakes, at any rate in the early days of his tenure'). The character of the hand makes it unlikely that the Vindolanda fragment is a literary text, but might it be a documentary narrative of some actual engagement in this region, written in a vivid historic present tense? Such things are known in papyri from Egypt – for example, in a fragment of a Greek papyrus of *c.* AD 50–100, which describes an engagement in the eastern desert between Roman soldiers and the desert-dwellers. The contemptuous term *Brittunculi*, which is a recognisable diminutive formation but has not occurred before, suggests no great sympathy for the subjects of Roman rule. Alternatively, it may be that local commanders were considering the suitability of the Britons for recruitment into the local units – there were certainly British units already in existence and serving in other provinces by *c.* AD 100. The soldiers of the Batavian or Tungrian units will have established local connections with natives. The natural explanation of the military diploma mentioned above that the recipient was a Gaul (or perhaps the son of a Tungrian veteran) who settled at Vindolanda, with a locally acquired wife and children, after his discharge.[23]

Citation of evidence at this humble level serves to emphasise the need to consider how best to make progress from these minutiae to matters of more general significance. One means of doing this is to consider what the tablets tell us about the relationship between what we can see in this peripheral region and the central structures of the military command and executive of the empire. Needless to say, no tablet provides us with a written instruction from the emperor, be it Domitian, Trajan or Hadrian. Who, then, determined the details of policy and organisation in a frontier region? If the notion of a centralised 'high command', a coherent view of the military needs of the various frontier regions of the empire and a perfected method of meeting those needs can ever have been envisaged, it is surely time to take a different view. The rhetoric of the second-century sophist Aelius Aristides of Smyrna in his speech 'To Rome' might imply such a role for the emperor, but that is highly idealised.[24] Even references which we do have in our texts to a trip to Gaul, or even to Rome,[25] do not give us that vital link to the nerve centre of imperial policy. For all practical purposes, given the slowness of communication with Rome, the crucial figure was the provincial governor but the evidence for the activities of our Vindolanda units suggests, as we shall see, a considerable degree of regional decentralisation with a good deal of initiative in the hands of local auxiliary commanders like Cerialis. There was perhaps little or no day-to-day direction from legionary headquarters at York, still less from the provincial governor, though he remains a pervasively powerful background figure and is mentioned in several texts. Several items assure us of the existence of regular communication: the detachment of troops from the Tungrian unit serving as *singulares legati* (the governor's bodyguard), probably in the office of a legionary legate, the presence of a letter sent to the governor's groom (*equisio consularis*) in London and brought back to Vindolanda, the note to Priscinus assuring him that letters which he has despatched to the governor with two soldiers from the Tungrian cohort had reached Ribchester and been sent on their way; several notes which mention the despatch or return of individual soldiers.[26] All of which depends on the infrastructure of communication which had already been established in the Brigantian region, primarily in the shape of a system of trunk-roads; an account of expenses probably incurred on a journey contains entries mentioning Catterick (Cataractonium), Binchester (Vinovia) and Aldborough (Isurium) and reminds us of the direction of one of the arterial routes in the north-east.[27] This emphasises that the viability of the frontier zone depends not merely on communication within that zone but on the maintenance of links with the region to the south which itself retained substantial occupying forces.

To supplement the physical evidence for the communication network, we should look at the nexus of professional, social and psychological links which pervade all levels of the establishment. At the time when Flavius Cerialis was prefect at Vindolanda, the governor of Britain was one Neratius Marcellus, attested in office by a diploma of AD 103. He was one of a pair of brothers of high attainment (the other was a distinguished jurist and public servant) with good connections at the imperial court. The position and influence of such a man was used by Pliny the Younger to procure a military tribunate for Suetonius, the biographer of the emperors, which was transferred, when the latter decided that, after all, he did not want it, to one of his relatives.[28] Flavius Cerialis has left us a draft of a letter, probably written in his own hand, in which he uses an intermediary named Crispinus, perhaps a high-ranking officer, to secure access to the governor. In the letter he makes an unfortunately fragmentary observation the sense of which must be something like 'he (sc. the governor) therefore offers (?) the opportunity now of . . . the talents (?) of your friends through his presence, of which you have, I know, very many, thanks to him. Now, in whatever way you wish, fulfil what I expect of you and and . . . so furnish me with very many friends that thanks to you I may be able to enjoy a pleasant period of military service.'[29] History, or rather archaeology, has not preserved Crispinus' response, though it may still lie among our illegible fragments. We do not know what Cerialis wanted to achieve by this (a transfer or a promotion?), but he might eventually have achieved the desired contact. A brief letter from two fellow-officers, Niger and Brocchus, sends generalised good wishes for Cerialis' success and concludes confidently – either by way of hope or warning – that he will soon meet the governor, '*consulari n(ostro) utique maturius occurres*'.[30] Good progress for a Batavian who was perhaps the first Roman citizen in his family, but perhaps to be expected among the officer class. The attempt by Claudius Karus to assist Brigionus by recommending him to Cerialis and, in turn, the centurion Annius Equester, shows the system working at a lower level and it is significant that it provided, at least in theory, a means of access for the lowly.[31] We should perhaps not assume too readily that the humble could approach the local people only in the lower reaches of the hierarchy. However remote the powerful figures were, a person of modest station could still draft a letter or petition to someone whom he addresses as *tuam maiestatem*, a term which could hardly be applied to any lesser personage than the provincial governor.[32]

The presence of these Tungrians and Batavians in northern Britain in *c.* AD 100 is testimony to the huge investment, political, economic and cultural, which Rome had already made in northern Gaul and was in the process of making in northern Britain. The acquisition of a Gallic or Germanic clientele provided the necessary personnel for the introduction of a stable and loyal military presence in the newly acquired region. At the officer level, people like Flavius Cerialis exemplify the acculturation of the élites of the fringe regions who had much to gain from acceptance of and compliance with Roman suzerainty. It is not merely a matter of numbers, for the symbols of Roman dominance were as powerful as, if not more powerful than, their mere numerical strength. Roman rule represented a relatively permanent and organised system which had an immense power to accumulate and absorb the local institutions. The evidence of the Vindolanda texts discussed in the following chapters illustrates as much as anything the power of those symbols and the depth of the investment. As so often, the contemporary historian Tacitus enables us to see the point with absolute clarity. Just before the last and greatest victory of Agricola, at Mons Graupius, he has the British chieftain Calgacus make a speech in which he prophesies that the Gauls, Germans and Britons in Agricola's army will desert the Roman standards to join their threatened British brethren: *agnoscent Britanni suam causam, recordabuntur Galli priorem libertatem, tam deserent illos ceteri Germani, quam nuper Usipi . . .* ('the Britons will acknowledge their own cause, the Gauls will remember their earlier freedom, the other Germans will abandon them as the Usipi did recently . . .').[33] But that was precisely what they did not do. Had Calgacus been able to express his disappointment after the event Tacitus might have thought it appropriate to have him say simply: *nimium multi Batavi linguam Latinam habent* ('too many Batavians speak Latin').

NOTES

1 For a basic historical account see Frere (1987), chs 5–7; for Agricola, most recently Hanson (1987).

2 E.g. Burnham and Johnson (1979), Blagg and King (1984), Millett (1990); for summaries of recent developments in research see Todd (ed. 1989), R. J. F. Jones (1991).

3 *Hist.*1.2. For Agricola see Hanson (1987).

4 G. D. B. Jones (1990).

5 See Breeze and Dobson (1985).

6 **1**; this tablet is made of oak (information from R. E. Birley).

7 See Smeesters (1977), *VRR* II, 5–9.

8 *VRR* II, 6–7.

9 See Frere and Wilkes (1989), Maxfield (1986). For the military units and their subdivisions see Appendix I, below.

10 See G. D. B. Jones (1990).

11 Pannonian revolt: Cassius Dio, 55.29–34, Velleius Paterculus 2.110–15, cf. Mócsy in Hartley and Wacher (ed. 1983), 169–78. Rhine mutiny, Tacitus, *Ann.* 1.31–44. Florus and Sacrovir, Tacitus, *Ann.* 3.40–6.

12 E.g. Cordonovi (or -vae, or -via), **24**.2–3; Briga, **10**.38, **22**.c.v.2; Ulucium (?), **5** α.4.

13 It is instructive to compare the remarks on the eastern frontier in Isaac (1992), 102–13.

14 *Tab. Vindol.* II 159.

15 *Tab. Vindol.* II 225–90.

16 Third cohort: **29**.back, *Tab. Vindol.* II 263. Letters: *Tab. Vindol.* II 263.00. Batavian cohorts on the Danube, Strobel (1987), *VRR* II, 7–8.

17 Letter to Priscinus: **23**. Sabinus from Trier: **8**.i.4. Diploma: *RMD* II 97. Letter to a decurion: **24**. Vardulli: **7**.13, cf. *CIL* 16.43, 51. Legionaries: **6**.22 (for an early legionary tombstone from Carvoran see *RIB* 1826).

18 Mons Graupius: Tacitus, *Agr.*36.1. Special relationship: Tacitus, *Germ.* 29.2–3; it is to be noted that Tacitus writes *c.* AD 100 as if the special relationship were still in force and

there is no good reason to think that this is not the case. Conquest of Britain: Hassall (1970). Revolt: Tacitus, *Hist.* 4.12–37, 54–79, 5.14–26. Continued presence in Britain: Strobel (1987), cf. Tacitus, *Hist.* 4. 18, 20, 56, 70. Command by nobles, Tacitus, *Hist.* 4.12. Claudius Labeo, Tacitus, *Hist.* 4.18.

19 Arminius: Tacitus, *Ann.* 1.56–71, 2.5–26. Pannonians: Mócsy in Hartley and Wacher (ed. 1983), 169–78. Florus and Sacrovir: Tacitus, *Ann.* 3.40–6.

20 Petillius Vindex: *CIL* 16.43 (AD 98). *civitas Batavorum*, *CIL* 13.8771.

21 *Tab. Vindol.* II 304. Colchester: *ILS* 2740. *censitor Brittonum Anavion[ensium]*: *ILS* 1338 (perhaps in south-west Scotland, see *PNRB* 249–50). An equestrian officer receives a census declaration in Arabia, Lewis (1989), no.16.

22 **19**.i.5–9. For another *centurio regionarius* in Britain see *RIB* 152 (Bath, probably second century) and cf. *RIB* 583, 587 (Ribchester).

23 **3**. Officer in Egypt: *P. Abinn.* 2.6–7. Papyrus: E. G. Turner, *JRS* 40 (1950), 57–9 (for the suggestion that the Vindolanda text might be literary see A. R. Birley (1991), 99, note 54). Recruitment of Britons: Hassall (1978), 45, cf. Tacitus, *Agr.* 29.2, 32.1. Diploma: *RMD* II 97.

24 J. H. Oliver, *The ruling power* (American Philosophical Society, Philadelphia, 1953).

25 Gaul, **20**.i.3–4. Rome, *Tab. Vindol.* II 283.4.

26 *singulares*, **1**.5–6. Letter to groom, **28**. Letter to Priscinus, **23**. Soldiers' movements: *Tab. Vindol.* II 252, 300, 345.

27 *Tab. Vindol.* II 185.

28 Diploma: *CIL* 16.48. Tribunate: Pliny, *Ep.* 3.8. Cf. A. R. Birley (1991), 95–100.

29 **15**.15–24.

30 **18**.ii.9–11.

31 **19**.

32 **33**.i.4–5.

33 Tacitus, *Agr.* 32.3.

4

THE ROMAN ARMY

DOCUMENTING THE ARMY

The Roman army was by far the largest international organisation of classical antiquity. In about AD 100 its total strength was probably around 300,000, more or less equally divided between legions and auxiliary units, unevenly spread over a vast area stretching from the Tyne to the Euphrates. As an empire-wide institution, it inevitably attracts the attention of those who look for common or unifying features in this vast and culturally diverse agglomeration of subject peoples and regions. Types of unit, fighting methods, internal organisation, rates of pay and donatives, official religious observances are all areas in which we expect to find some degree of uniformity. The same applies, to a certain extent, to the general character of its activities: fighting, of course, but also building and engineering, garrison and policing duties, supervision of the commissariat, transportation and communications.[1] Finally, and not least important, the fact that throughout the empire its official language of operation was Latin, even, for instance, in Egypt, where the business of the civil administration was conducted entirely in Greek.

Beneath this broad and superficial uniformity, however, one might expect to find some degree of diversity, dictated by the nature of the units, the geographical characteristics of the region, the social, economic and cultural organisation of the subject population. Auxiliary units of Batavian infantry or cavalry differed from Palmyrene archers; the business of feeding and maintaining the army in Britain might require a different organisation from that in Africa or Egypt. The accretion of new evidence for the army of Roman Britain offers the opportunity to flesh out the regional history which is in itself the indispensable basis of any appreciation of what 'romanisation' really means; only when this has been done can we proceed to attempt, by comparison with our similar documentary evidence from elswhere (principally Egypt and Syria), to discern common structural features.

Our literary evidence for the general organisation of the army is less helpful than one might hope. The only writer who gives details of the sort which are relevant to what we find in our Vindolanda texts is Vegetius, but his usefulness is limited since he wrote his *Epitoma rei militaris* in the mid-fourth century and explicitly with reference to the legions.[2] The papyri and ostraka from Egypt and papyri from the site of Doura-Europos on the Euphrates in Syria give us a large number of official documents of various kinds. The Egyptian documents come from a variety of sources and are thus not locally or chronologically coherent; Doura-Europos has produced an archive unified in time and place, but diverse in two respects from Vindolanda for it relates to the third century, and to a unit (the Twentieth Cohort of Palmyrene Archers) stationed on the eastern frontier. More recently, the publication of ostraka from Bu Njem in Libya has given us some information for the Roman army of Africa in the mid-third century AD which actually shows striking parallels for some of our Vindolanda texts.[3] As far as Vindolanda is concerned, there are two great bonuses; one is that it gives us evidence for the north-western sector of the empire whilst virtually all of our comparative material comes from the other end of the empire; the other is that it bears upon the role and organisation of the auxiliary units in contrast to the bulk of our evidence which is relevant to the legions.

There is one universal feature of army organisation which Vegetius does stress – the quantity of documentation involved. He supplies a note of the clerical staff employed in the legionary *tabularium*, for which there must have been a smaller, auxiliary equivalent:

> Totius enim legionis ratio, sive obsequiorum sive militarium munerum sive pecuniae, cotidie adscribitur actis maiore prope diligentia quam res annonaria vel civilis polyptychis adnotatur. cotidianas etiam in pace vigilias, item excubitum sive agrarias omnibus centuriis vicissim milites faciunt: ut ne quis contra iustitiam praegravetur aut alicui praestetur immunitas, nomina eorum, qui vices suas fecerunt, brevibus inseruntur. quando quis commeatum acceperit, vel quot dierum, adnotatur in brevibus. tunc enim difficile commeatus dabatur nisi causis iustissimis adprobatis.

> For the administration of the entire legion, including special services, military services and money, is recorded daily in the Acts with one might say greater exactitude than records of military and civil taxation are noted down in official files. Daily even in peacetime, soldiers take it in turns from all centuries and 10-man sections to do night-watch duties,

> sentry duty, and outpost duties. The names of those who have done their turn are entered in lists so that no-one is unjustly overburdened or given exemption. When anyone receives leave of absence and for how many days, it is noted down in lists. For in antiquity it was very difficult to be given leave unless for very good approved reasons.[4]

The amount of paperwork was, no doubt, enormous, so much so that it could be useful as a yard-stick in measuring the wealth of a probably fictional Alexandrian merchant of the third century AD named Firmus – he was said to own so many books that he could keep the whole army supplied with the raw materials needed for its paperwork.[5] The antecedents of the military bureaucracy must surely have existed in the late Republic, but it would be reasonable to guess that the developed form evolved in the Augustan period, as a concomitant of Augustus' army reforms and the introduction of the *aerarium militare* (military treasury). Even a cursory survey of the whole corpus of Roman military records on papyrus might well suggest that we can have only the tip of the iceberg, comprising lists of soldiers, duty rosters, pay records, some accounts and some official correspondence. Some idea of what we have lost can be obtained from the calculation that in the period from Augustus to Diocletian the army bureaucracy would have produced at least 225,000,000 individual soldiers' pay-records, of which three survive in a reasonable state of preservation.[6]

Virtually all of these surviving military documents, emanating from the army in Roman Egypt and the unit at Doura-Europos, give us some insight into the official records which the military organisation generated. At Vindolanda, however, we have a great range of texts which happen to have been discarded in a relatively short period of time in the area of the *praetorium* and the later barrack-block and workshop, perhaps therefore destined for the files of the commanding officers and other individuals rather than the unit's record-office. It is significant, therefore, that there is such a bulk of documentation outside the *principia* (headquarters building) and the *tabularium* (record-office) of the unit and interesting to have an insight into the range of documentation which might be generated in an auxiliary fort. Taking our lead from Vegetius, we need to consider the nature and content of this documentation before we move on to discuss the range and coherence of the army's activities in the region.

Several of our official reports are concerned with recording the strength and organisation of the unit or units at Vindolanda. As we have seen, the strength report of the Tungrian cohort is cast in a relatively standard format giving an overall total, the numbers of those absent and their locations, those present and, as a sub-category, those who were unfit for service. A comparison with similar strength reports on papyrus is instructive. A contemporary report from the province of Moesia, which paradoxically turned up in Egypt, shows a similar heading, though fuller and more formal than that of the Vindolanda text, and places groups detached for duty with the governor and the procurator at the head of the list of those inside the province; various other groups are recorded in detached garrisons and on expeditions to fetch or guard supplies.[7] A similar report from the mid-second century, recording the strength of a cohort stationed in the Thebaid, describes itself as a *pridianum* (a report made *pridie Kalendas*, on the last day of a month or year).[8] The date of the Vindolanda text, however, is *xv K(alendas) Iunias* (18 May) which does not suggest any obvious annual, monthly or bi-monthly pattern of reporting. All known texts of this general type, however, show minor variations of detail, and the Vindolanda report might suggest that such returns were frequently made to the unit commander and formed the basis for compiling official and more formal reports which would be sent at fixed intervals to the provincial headquarters. The notion that this is an interim report made for the commanding officer is supported by the impression that in several places the numbers at the right-hand end of the lines are rather crushed in, as if they were added after the main outline had been drafted. That there were checks of the subdivisions too is perhaps suggested by a fragment of a letter from the prefect Cerialis in which he seems to be instructing an absent member of his own unit to come to Vindolanda for a *numeratio* (count), probably of a century or of centurions.[9]

A similar conclusion seems to emerge from a comparison of some other Vindolanda texts recording activities of various groups of soldiers with the duty rosters of the Third Legion (Cyrenaica) from Egypt and ostraka from Bu Njem. There are two reports from Vindolanda which begin with a date heading followed by a list of assignments of various groups. One of these is dated 7 March and records 30 builders, working on a *hospitium* (residence) under the direction of a *medicus* (a doctor or a medical orderly), 18 men quarrying or transporting stone and another group getting clay for work on the hurdles or fences of the camp. Another report of 25 April records 343 men assigned to the workshops (*fabricae*) and then a list of smaller groups from this total: 12 cobblers or leather-workers, 18 builders (*structores*) working on the bath-house, and at least 7 other similar assignments for which the entries are not fully preserved. A third text, probably of this type, records parties of 46 and 18 men respectively.

Although it is not possible to determine the precise size of the garrison at Vindolanda in Period 3, from which these reports come, the 343 men in the workshops must have represented a significant proportion of it. A fourth, very fragmentary text may also report activities in the workshops, for it appears to record the names of men, followed by a trade and the century to which they belonged; some of these seem to be specialist craftsmen making weapons.[10]

Some features of these texts might be noted. First, they lack a certain formality, though the format is broadly standard. The headings consist only of a date and there is little sign of standardisation; two of the lists use the unmarked abbreviation *h* for *h(omines)*, which is less common than *m* for *m(ilites)* in texts of this type; they are certainly all written in different hands. In fact, the documents themselves do not tell us what they are. The dates, in so far as we have them, do not seem significant, not falling at the beginning or end of a month or year. They look very much like working notes from which the more formal records of unit strength and duties might be compiled. The legionary records from Egypt include both detailed notes of what individual soldiers were doing and complementary numerical summaries of groups. We have, of course, no way of knowing how frequently or regularly such notes were made and submitted to the commanding officer, a procedure which their presence in the *praetorium* at Vindolanda would suggest. It is, however, noteworthy that the Latin ostraka from Bu Njem supply an almost exact parallel for the format of the reports and point to the broad prevalence of procedures of this kind in the army.[11]

The general paucity of evidence of this kind means that it is hardly surprising that entirely new types of document turn up from time to time and there is one such group which is evidently standard at Vindolanda but unlike anything found elsewhere. There are 27 separate fragments of documents which, taken together, allow us to reconstruct a report of a formulaic kind, with minor variations. The text begins with a date (the individual examples again suggest no obvious pattern), followed by the phrase *renuntium cohortis viiii Batavorum*; *renuntium* must mean 'report' (though this is a very rare usage) and in all the examples where the identity of the unit can be read, it is the Ninth Cohort of Batavians. Then we have the phrase *omnes ad loca* (or *locum*) *q(ui) videbunt et impedimenta* ('all are at their posts and they will also see to the baggage'). This is followed by the names of the reporting officers and in some cases also the name of the person who actually delivered the report. It was clearly the *optiones* (second in command to the centurion in a century) who were responsible for making these regular routine reports, the purpose of which may simply be to check and record that soldiers are at their posts or assignments (*loca*), whether inside or outside the fort.[12] It is striking that the texts are all in different hands and this, along with the curious formulae and/or idiosyncrasies, suggests that there was an exemplar which the individual *optiones* followed in making routine reports to the commander. The reports might, of course, refer to detachments under the authority of *optiones* (and sometimes *curatores*) at outposts or fortlets, as well as to the personnel within the fort. Though the period and the organisation are very different, these reports do evoke comparison with the description which the historian Polybius gives of the system of inspecting the guard-posts in the legionary army of the second century BC; the soldiers responsible for the inspection have to prove that they have completed the rounds and that the posts are manned by producing written tokens (*tesserae*) from each of the posts inspected.[13]

The great rosters from Doura-Europos and the payroll accounts from Egypt assure us that careful records were kept of individuals too, but Vindolanda has not yet yielded anything comparable. There is one fragmentary list of names but it tells us very little.[14] Individual soldiers were allowed to take leave (*commeatus*), as is well known, and our name-lists could, for example, be records of individuals to whom leave had been given. That lists and records of individuals were kept by commanding officers is only to be expected and is implied in a letter from a prefect to a colleague in which he says *te rogo frater continuo illos expungas* ('I ask, brother, that you immediately strike them off the list').[15]

Be that as it may, Vindolanda does supply important new evidence on the details of the system of granting leave. A handful of fragmentary letters shows that there was a regular procedure by which applications for leave were made at Vindolanda; we are surely entitled to assume that this was a general practice, even though the Vindolanda texts are unique.[16] Some, perhaps almost all, belong with the papers of Cerialis. The letters do not appear to carry a formal address of the kind which we find in personal letters. They are almost formulaic, though with some variation in the order of the elements: a name perhaps followed by the identifying subdivision of the unit (century or *turma*), followed by *rogo domine (Cerialis) me dignum habeas cui des commeatum* ('I ask, my lord (Cerialis), that you consider me worthy to be granted leave'). In one case this is certainly followed by the place-name Coris, the locative form of Coria which must surely be Corbridge, with the name of the individual coming after that. Two others appear to mention places, and one of these perhaps also specifies a reason for wanting to go, but the place-names are unknown. There is no sign that the applicants ask for a specific number of days, but there may have been a standard grant; alternatively the commander might have decided on the number of days when he knew where the applicant was going. We have a reference in a papyrus from Egypt telling us that a soldier expected to be able to return home from Arabia during his leave. Our Vindolanda soldiers might have been more restricted in range: Corbridge is very near to Vindolanda, but we should perhaps not assume too readily that they were denied the opportunity to return to their homeland in northern Gaul. In view of the fact that these requests must have come from a level below the officer class it is interesting that they are not 'form letters' but are written in different hands, and in this respect they contrast with a related document from Egypt, a chit granting leave, in which a second hand has written the name of the individual in a space left blank for that purpose.[17]

Records of cash, commodities, and transactions were kept no less scrupulously than those of military personnel. Documents on papyrus provide clear testimony of detailed accounting procedures for military pay and other financial activities. Legions had batteries of clerks, the much smaller auxiliary units correspondingly fewer. The military service of Pliny the Younger, we know, consisted of a six-month legionary tribunate during which he audited the accounts of auxiliary units in the province of Syria.[18] Overall control in Britain will have ultimately been vested in the emperor's procurator, but this does not surface directly in our Vindolanda texts, despite the large number which concern various aspects of financial control. One difficulty which we face in interpreting the accounts is to determine which are relevant to the administration of the fort and the units as a whole and which to the domestic administration of the *praetorium* – it is hardly surprising given the location of the finds that a significant proportion seems to reflect the latter and the details will be discussed in Chapter 6. We should not draw too clear a line of demarcation between accounts and transactions in the fort as a whole and those in the *praetorium* as if the former were official and the latter were private in the sense that they stood outside the military establishment as a whole. In fact, it is precisely the variety of the documentation which evokes a picture of a military community in which the *familia* (household) of the commanding officer was central and integral.

Several items of considerable interest offer evidence of broad relevance and give a good idea of the range of our documentation. First, an account of small cash sums over a period of a few days in July of an unspecified year is headed *reditus castelli* ('revenues of the fort'). The fort must be Vindolanda, the total sum is comparatively small (something over 80 *denarii*), but its mere existence in this form is of great interest. That the fort could compute revenues in cash on a daily basis shows money coming in regularly, perhaps from sales of surplus supplies or goods manufactured in the camp. Second, there is an account which is the only document in the entire collection to offer us clear evidence of a date, somewhat fortuitous, in fact, since the sequence of entries happens to run across the beginning of a new year and refers to the consulship of Calpurnius Piso and Vettius Bolanus (AD 111). The items accounted for include *cervesa* (Celtic beer) and *clavi caligares* (nails for boots), salt, pork and goat-meat and they are dispensed to and through individuals who might be slaves. Third, a longer and more detailed account, from the later part of the period, is written in three columns and arranged by centuries, then by the names of individual soldiers against which are recorded commodities and sums in cash. Some of the names are conspicuously Germanic (though several are not elsewhere attested) and we are certainly dealing with the ordinary rankers here: Tagarminis, Gambax, son of Tappo, Ammius, Messor, Huep . . ., Tullio, Butimas. The list of commodities is a varied one including *piper* (pepper), *sudaria* (napkins or towels), *sebum* (tallow, probably used as soap), *coturnus* (a rustic boot), *sagaciae* (cloaks) and *superariae* (overcoats). All these are followed by sums in cash (generally small) which suggests that they were purchases of 'non-essential' items made by ordinary soldiers from the monies left to them after the standard deductions had been made from their pay. What is not clear is whether these items were paid for by deduction from deposits (as for instance might have been the case with the payments made for weapons and equipment) or whether cash actually changed hands. But two deductions seem permissible: first, that the range of goods available to ordinary soldiers was considerable and second that the camp, in effect, operated an internal cash-commodity market in which purchases were carefully recorded. The evidence discussed in the next chapter shows the variety of goods and activities for which accounts are kept at Vindolanda. There is no reason to believe that Vindolanda was unique in this respect – quite the reverse.[19]

Finally, three examples will serve to show that the meticulous recording of commodities was also carried out in the *praetorium*. A long, daily account of foodstuffs for June of an unspecified year was thought, when it was first published, to be an official record of dispensation of supplies. It now seems much more likely that it records items, including *cervesa* (Celtic beer), *hordeum* (barley) and *vinum* (wine), used in the officer's household. Some of the entries carry the notation *per Privatum*; Privatus is a typical servile name and that the account was kept by slaves is suggested by the fact that it uses the words *dominus* and *domini* which probably refer to the head of the house and his family. A second, shorter account is a cash account for the purchase of food, including different kinds of meat, and here there is a notation which may well stand for *in praetorio*. It is perhaps to this context that we should assign a simple arithmetical calculation of an unnamed commodity, perhaps of a liquid variety: *]vii K(alendas) Ian(uarias) in singulos dies (sextarii) iiii sunt dies xlii modii x s(emis)* ('26 December (?), 4 *sextarii* per day, total for 42 days, 10½ *modii*').[20]

THE ACTIVITIES OF THE ARMY

The characteristics and activities of the Roman army as a fighting force, for subjugation and for maintaining the peace in the provinces and frontier regions, are matters of great interest and importance. That fighting, military manoeuvres and training do not surface directly in our texts from Vindolanda is presumably due only to the fact that this side of the picture is liable to be less comprehensively documented than the organisational side and more particularly so outside the official record-office of the fort which might be expected to contain intelligence reports and official despatches. Although the period of three decades before the building of Hadrian's Wall was far from being simply a time of peace, the activities which we can observe in the Vindolanda texts are, in effect, peacetime ones and not the less informative for that. There are clear signs that a highly developed military technology was already firmly in place.

First, building. It is evident that the personnel of auxiliary units did not simply wait for the legions to do this, but took responsibility for a great deal of it themselves. The reports which contain details of work-parties record builders and plasterers, groups dealing with lead, clay, cement, burning lime (presumably in lime-kilns, perhaps referred to simply as *furnaces*, ovens) and perhaps making hurdles or fences. The fort at Vindolanda underwent at least one major modification and several minor ones during our period and these are presumably reflected in such activities. Apart from the workshops themselves (*fabricae*) three specific buildings are mentioned in our reports. A party of 18 builders is assigned to the bath-house (*balneum*), the presence of which is reflected also in an account mentioning a *balniator* (bathman) named Vitalis; the subsequent reference in the report to *plumbum* (lead) is more likely than not to be connected with this facility. Another entry in the same report mentions the *valetudinarium*, the hospital, whose existence might have been inferred from the presence of the *aegri* and *volnerati* listed in the strength report of the Tungrian cohort. The third building is the *hospitium*, a residence which might perhaps have served as a guest-house, a facility whose importance is underlined by a number of letters which refer to people visiting other posts or stopping en route to some other destination.[21]

For these operations, collection and transport of the raw materials were vital and much was no doubt carried out by military personnel rather than civilian traders. There is a text which refers to the storage of wood and timber (*lignum et materies*), another mentions wood which has been purchased (*lignis emtis*).[22] The writing-tablets themselves are presumably a by-product of this, but stone figures much more prominently and compares well with the abundant evidence of the ostraka from Mons Claudianus in the eastern desert of Egypt which show intensive military control and supervision of these important stone-quarries.[23] One letter from Vindolanda notes the despatch of wagons to a prefect named Vocusius Africanus, another refers to the urgent need for delivery of lime (*calx*), *quas rogo continuo iubeas onerari ut primo mane nobis iter faciant* ('I ask you to order them to be loaded without pause so that they (sc. vehicles or mules?) may make their way (?) to us early in the morning'); a third makes detailed arrangements for the transport of stone, probably under the supervision of a centurion named Vocontius. Given the constant need for new building in this area at this time it is perhaps unnecessary and too early to connect any of this directly with the construction of Hadrian's Wall, which began in the early 120s, and it is noteworthy that there were sources of clay and stone very close to the fort at Vindolanda.[24]

Second, manufacture. There is no doubt that the legionary workshops were much concerned with the manufacture of weapons; a papyrus of the second or third century from Egypt shows small groups of men working in the workshop of the Second Legion (Traiana) on a whole range of weapons including bows, shields, broadswords and catapults.[25] Nevertheless, it does look as if the Vindolanda auxiliary units may have had an important role to play in the supply of their own weaponry. One fragmentary text appears to use the general term for craftsmen (*fabri*) along with the specialist term *scutarius* (shield-maker) and perhaps a reference to swords; an account records a *scutarius* probably named Lucius. There is some direct archaeological evidence for metal-working (at least in the form of repair) at Vindolanda in this period. The presence of ovens or kilns and the reference to lead have already been noted and it may be relevant that two accounts mention purchases of iron (*ferrum*); the raw mineral resources lay near at hand. The letter of Octavius begins by mentioning a relatively large quantity of sinew (*nervum*), 100 lbs; one of the uses to which this material could be put was the construction of catapults. The construction of vehicles is the central concern in a letter from Metto to Advectus, which includes in the list of items despatched *modiola* (hubs), *axses carrarios* (axles for carts), *radia* (spokes), *sessiones* (seats); this implies that the constituent parts were manufactured elsewhere and sent to Vindolanda for assembly. We do not know who or where Metto was, which is unfortunate. The name (which is otherwise unattested) does not help, beyond suggesting an origin in the north-western provinces. We cannot be certain whether he was a Gaul or a Briton, soldier or civilian, but we can say that he writes (or least can conduct his business) in decent Latin and his activities were wholly or partly necessitated and supported by the military presence; there is no reason to suppose that Advectus and the unit at Vindolanda will have been the only recipients of his goods.[26]

Among the general range of equipment which soldiers needed, leatherware and footwear bulk large at Vindolanda and form a significant proportion of the surviving artefacts in the pre-Hadrianic area.[27] The groups recorded as working in the *fabricae* include cobblers or leather-workers (*sutores*) (pl. 1). The letter of Octavius is important in this respect because it refers to the transport of hides in bulk, as well as to the sale and (apparently) the processing, and this can be supplemented by the letter of Metto which concludes by saying that he has sent five goatskins to Advectus, who is presumably at Vindolanda. Octavius' reference to the presence of hides at Catterick is of particular interest since that site has produced evidence for tanning which has identified it as the major producer of leather for the army in this region. The record of *clavi caligares* (nails for boots) in a Vindolanda account certainly implies local facilities for repair of the finished product whether or not the metal-working and tanning were carried out on the spot.[28]

Similarly, although there is plenty of information concerning a varied range of textiles and clothing, it is difficult to find direct evidence for its manufacture at Vindolanda; the record of about 38 lbs of wool in an account may, however, provide strong circumstantial evidence for some textile manufacture in or very near to the fort.[29]

Much of the most detailed and important information in this category is concerned with the supply system which kept the army of the frontier regions fed, clothed and furnished with other necessities, and military personnel were naturally at the centre of this. The provision of basic foodstuffs for a fort containing several hundred people was obviously a major operation, and the evidence from Vindolanda offers selective and suggestive details rather than a sight of large-scale operations such as we find, for instance, in a book of several dozen individual receipts for hay-money from members of a cavalry unit in second-century Egypt.[30] Nonetheless, one of the most informative of the Vindolanda accounts shows the distribution of a total of over 300 *modii* of wheat to various individuals and groups and for various purposes which can hardly be interpreted as a standard issue of basic rations to ordinary soldiers. There is a loan, an issue to a *beneficiarius* (probably the adjutant of the prefect of the cohort), to legionary soldiers, to oxherds and to others in charge of livestock. We do not know the position of the person who kept this account, but the occurrence of the words *mihi* ('to myself'), *tibi* ('to you') and *patri* ('to father') perhaps suggests a family business involving a father and two brothers. The recipients and the functions recorded must be part of the military establishment and the use of the phrase *in ussus* [*sic*] *suos* ('for his own use') in one entry does suggest a distinction between personal and official use. This gives an added interest to the evidence for oxherds and other supervisors of livestock (*bubulcari*, *ad porcos*, *ad iuvencos*) and implies a direct responsibility for agricultural land and the production of foodstuffs in the region of the fort; this will account for some of the cereals and meat consumed, as well as by-products such as *lardum* (pork-fat) and *axungia* (axle-grease). There is no reason to deny that, as elsewhere, the basic needs will have been met by a mixture of direct production, purchase and requisition. A fragmentary official document may well refer to members of a *turma* going off to collect barley, much used as animal feed, and in one of the letters to Cassius Saecularis, the writer refers to the purchase of barley (*hordeum commercium*), perhaps implying commercial relations with the native Britons. Another letter probably refers to the sale of the cereal known as *braces*. Octavius too wishes to buy grain, asking his correspondent Candidus for the money to enable him to do so; his reference to a previous purchase of 5000 *modii* makes it clear that he is dealing with supplies for a considerable number of people. He also handles *braces*, a cereal known to have been used in the production of Celtic beer, which figures prominently in our accounts. That the brewing itself might well have been done at or near Vindolanda is strongly suggested by a reference to a *cervesarius* (brewer) named Atrectus.[31]

There are many other references to food, clothing and equipment of various kinds which are better discussed in the general context of social and economic life at Vindolanda (Chapter 5, below). The provision of clothing, in particular, is mentioned mainly in individual transactions. One account, however, which records ordinary tunics and cloaks (*saga*, *palliola*, *tunicae*), as well as capes (*umeralia*), in batches of up to about 15 in number, might, if it is not connected with the personnel in the *praetorium*, refer to provision of clothing for members of a *contubernium*.[32]

We may assume that, as in Egypt, soldiers will have been involved in the transport of such goods, as well as the acquisition of foodstuffs, such as salt, from further afield. If parties of soldiers went off to collect pay (*stipendium*), as they might have done, they could bring back other goods too, even if only incidentally. The several references in our correspondence to the despatch of soldiers to and from well-known forts like Catterick, York, Binchester, Ribchester and Carlisle, as well as further afield in Gaul, will account for some small-scale movement of goods, as well as for the delivery of the letters themselves. The production and the acquisition, by local purchase or import, of a wide variety of commodities raise the major issue of the effect of the army's activities on the surrounding region, in particular in the creation of a demand for goods which went beyond the bare subsistence of the military presence and the ability of the region to meet the increasing demands. As we have seen, the manufacturing capability of these units was considerable, but we can hardly envisage complete self-sufficiency in local manufacture of, for example, towels (*sudaria*), even less so in the case of some of the more luxurious items which are attested in the context of the *praetorium* and even the later buildings where the appearance of pepper, an expensive luxury item from the east, is very striking.[33]

Import on a considerable scale is surely indicated by this evidence, though we cannot test the hypothesis that there was a change in the balance of trade towards the end of the first century. Entrepreneurs and merchants must have thrived on the opportunities offered by the army. Of the two accounts which are labelled *ratio Gavonis* one, listing textile items and foodstuffs, may well belong to the *praetorium*. The same Gavo is probably mentioned in a letter to Flavius Genialis, perhaps one of the prefects at Vindolanda, as a purveyor of unspecified items. It has proved (and still proves) very difficult to find positive and unequivocal evidence for civilians engaging in commerce with the army at this time in the northern frontier region. Gavo could be one such, Atrectus the *cervesarius* might be another who belonged to a civilian entrepreneurial milieu which followed in the footsteps of the army. Some of the individuals who produced or are named in the accounts associated with the period of the barrack-block or the workshop might be soldiers and, if so, it is perhaps worth noting that is the *optiones* who are generally known to have been heavily involved in the organisation and transport of supplies. It is hard to resist the notion, however, that activities of this sort strongly suggest the early development of the civil settlement (*vicus* or *canabae*) next to the military establishment, housing the people who responded to the new social and economic demands created by the military presence.[34]

There is nothing in the Vindolanda tablets which will undermine the basic notion that the needs of the army were supplied by a combination of imports from continental Europe and exploitation of the *territorium* around the forts. Vintage wine and stilus tablets were certainly imported, beer, meat and wool locally produced. Whilst we cannot draw up a detailed balance-of-trade account, our texts do enable us to observe some of the ways in which the army organised the exploitation of the resources of the region – foodstuffs, timber, metal, and stone. That the army effectively exploited a very great range of materials is, of course, sufficiently clear from the archaeological evidence alone. What we can do, however, is cast some light on the range of artisanal and manufacturing activity with particular reference to the general question of the degree of decentralisation and self-sufficiency in the region. First, we have very clear evidence for the availability of a range of specialist skills in and around the auxiliary units which has hitherto been identified only in connection with legions. If we pause to reflect that the nearest legion to Vindolanda was at York, then we can rapidly appreciate the difference which this knowledge makes to our assessment of the spread of military technology. The building of the hospital, residence and other camp facilities in the work-details suggests that these auxiliary units were capable of major building works. Vindolanda had workshops and it is probable that it had the capacity to manufacture its own weaponry or at least some proportion of it. We can also confidently deduce the presence of facilities for processing or repairing a large range of goods and commodities, from shoes to beer; and for a transportation network which made it relatively easy to obtain what could not be produced locally. The coherence of that network is underlined by the evidence which suggests the extent to which units, parts of units and individuals were moved around. This invites us to think in terms of the coherence of the region in which transportation and despatch of supplies and commodities are crucial, even though they might pose problems, especially in the winter: Octavius writes to Candidus, probably in January, about getting a wagon-load of hides, *iam illec petissem nisi iumenta non curavi vexsare dum viae male sunt* ('I would have already been to collect them except that I did not care to injure the animals while the roads are bad').[35]

Beyond the immediate locality of the fort, the unit can draw on goods and commodities available elsewhere at greater or lesser distance. The trading area was a continuum, in which the English Channel was no great obstacle. The accounts we have examined suggest that, to some extent, at least, the fort operated its own budget with a degree of independence – things were not simply supplied from some central army store. One way in which we can document the range of communication is simply by cataloguing and flagging on the map the names of places which are mentioned in our Vindolanda texts (fig. 3). With two cautions, unfortunately: one, that in most cases we simply do not know the origin of letters sent to Vindolanda, and second, that there are several place-names which we cannot as yet identify. Within Britain, we are assured of Luguvalium (Carlisle), Coria (Corbridge), Bremetennacum (Ribchester), Cataractonium (Catterick), Vinovia (Binchester), Isurium (Aldborough), Eburacum (York) and Londinium. We can add Briga, which is unknown but must be very close to Vindolanda, and probably Curia Textoverdorum which is also in this region. Then there are Ulucium(?), to which someone applies to go on leave, and Cordonovi (or -vae or -via), the source of a gift of oysters which might be on the north Kent coast of the Thames estuary. Valentinus has made a trip to Gaul and we may have a reference to a visit (probably by a correspondent of Flavius Cerialis and perhaps therefore of reasonably high rank) to Rome.[36] Apart from London, all of the known British place-names listed are within the ambit of the northern military command, which is itself not surprising; nor is the fact that our list includes several of the most important strategic sites of Roman occupation. The road networks which linked these places began to develop in the Flavian period and were undoubtedly reasonably comprehensive by AD 100. When we move further afield, we can perhaps link the presence of a centurion of the Tungrian cohort in London with the survival of a letter at Vindolanda which had probably been sent to the governor's groom (*equisio consularis*) in London.[37]

Our Vindolanda evidence shows that above all it was the intensive use of the written word that enabled the army to function with coherence in a large geographical area in a way which simply would not have been possible without it (see Chapter 7). It is striking, for instance, that Octavius refers to written communication five times in the first half of his letter.[38] Not only is there a sub-stratum of official documentation which provides the officers with a running record of the state of their units, but also a developed system of authenticating and checking the movements and contacts between units and between the regional army and the 'central command' in the province. Given the degree of fragmentation, this is clearly the only way in which such large areas could be systematically controlled by such small numbers of troops. The logic of this argument is that documentation and written communication are structurally central to the whole system and these are features which we can certainly trace back to the Augustan period and probably the Caesarean; it enabled the imperial army to be far more than merely a defensive or an aggesssive fighting force. Given the gaps in our evidence, we cannot rigorously test the notion that the modes of official documentation (still less the activities which they represent) were standardised throughout the army. It is impossible to be sure how much initiative lay in the hands of individual local commanders, but there was surely some. Overall, however, it seems clear that even in newly acquired areas garrisoned (and to some extent commanded) by personnel from fringe areas of the empire the system of documentation and written communication was not a matter of gradual development; it was, so to speak, imposed from the centre and was integral to the whole structure. It is very far from being merely a by-product of the army's role in Rome's imperialistic designs.

Notes

1 For recent re-evaluations of the role of the army on the frontiers see Isaac (1992), Whittaker (1989).

2 See now Milner (1993).

3 The papyri from Egypt and Doura-Europos are collected and re-edited in *RMR*. Note also the important new ostraka from the quarry site of Mons Claudianus in Egypt's eastern desert: *O. Claud.* Bu Njem ostraka: *O. Bu Njem.*

4 Vegetius, *Epitoma rei militaris*, 2.19 (trans. Milner, 1993).

5 *Historia Augusta*, *Quad. Tyr.* 3.1–2.

6 The loss is calculated at *RMR*, p. 242. Surviving records: *RMR* 68, 70, M. A. Speidel (1992).

7 *RMR* 63.

8 Thomas and Davies (1977).

9 *Tab. Vindol.* II 242. The term *numeratio* clearly has a technical meaning and might refer to counting or, in a financial sense, payment or accounting. Here it might indicate regular or special payments made to centurions.

10 *Tab. Vindol.* II 156, **2**, *Tab. Vindol.* II 157, 160; on the latter cf. Bishop (1985).

11 *O. Bu Njem* 1–62.

12 *Tab. Vindol.* II 127–53, **4**. In September 1993 R. E. Birley kindly sent news of the discovery of a complete example of this type of report.

13 Polybius *Hist.* 6.34.7–36.9.

14 *Tab. Vindol.* II 161.

15 *Tab. Vindol.* II 345.

16 *Tab. Vindol.* II 166–77, **5**.

17 Trip from Arabia, *P. Mich.* VIII 466. Chit with blank space, *O. Flor.* 1.

18 Papyri, *RMR* 68–81. Clerks, Vegetius, *Epitoma rei militaris*, 2.19 (trans. Milner, 1993); note that Vegetius refers to the need for knowledge of *notae* (shorthand?) and

accounting, see below, p. 91. Pliny, *Ep.* 3.11.5, 7.31.2.

19 *reditus castelli*, *Tab. Vindol.* II 178. Dated account, *Tab. Vindol.* II 186. Three-column account, **9**. For comparable material from Carlisle see Tomlin (1992).

20 **10**, **11**, *Tab. Vindol.* II 205.

21 **2**. *balniator*, **7**.8. *aegri* etc., **1**.22–4. *hospitium*, *Tab. Vindol.* II 156.2–3.

22 *Tab. Vindol.* II 215 **7**.3.

23 *O. Claud.*

24 *Tab. Vindol.* II, 315, 314, 316. Clay and stone, see *VRR* I.

25 *ChLA* X 409.

26 *fabri* etc., *Tab. Vindol.* II 160. Lucius, **9**.ii.21. Metal-working, *VRR* I. *ferrum*, **8**.ii.15, *Tab. Vindol.* II 183.2. Letter of Octavius, **32**. Letter of Metto, **27**.

27 *VRR* III, 1–75.

28 *sutores*, **2**.2. Letter of Octavius, **32**.ii.15, iii.30–iv.41. Letter of Metto, **27**.ii.14. Catterick, Burnham and Wacher (1990), 111–7. *clavi caligares*, *Tab. Vindol.* II 186.7–8.

29 *VRR* III, 76–90. **12**.

30 *RMR* 76.

31 Wheat account, **6**. *lardum*, etc., **8**. *turma*, *Tab. Vindol.* II 159. Barley, *Tab. Vindol.* II 213 (for some other evidence for Britons see *VRR* II, 29). *braces*, *Tab. Vindol.* II 305. Octavius, **32**. Brewer, **8**.ii.14.

32 *Tab. Vindol.* II 207.

33 Collection of pay perhaps in **1**.14 (cf. Tomlin (1986)). Movement of soldiers, **32**, **23**, **20**. Supply and demand, see Fulford (1984), Breeze (1984). Pepper, **9**.i.4.

34 Accounts of Gavo, *Tab. Vindol.* II 207, **12**. Letter to Genialis, *Tab. Vindol.* II 218. *cervesarius*, **8**.ii.14. *optiones*, *RMR*, p. 311, 81.ii.5–12. *canabae* and *vici*, Casey (1982), G. D. B. Jones (1984).

35 **32**.ii.19–21.

36 Luguvalium, **19**.i.9. Coria, **1**.7. Bremetennacum, **23**.i.6. Cataractonium, **32**.ii.16. Vinovia, Isurium, *Tab. Vindol.* II 185.26, 23. Eburacum, Inv.no.86.575 (stylus tablet, unpublished). London, **28**.back 1, **1**.9. Briga, **10**.38, Curia Textoverdorum, **30**.back 1. Ulucium, **5** α.4. Cordonovi (-vae, -via), **24**.i.2–3. Gaul, **20**.i.3–4. Rome, *Tab. Vindol.* II 283.4.

37 **1**.9, **28**.

38 **32**.i.5, ii.15, 16, 18, 19.

5

OFFICERS AND MEN, AND WOMEN

The Roman occupation of Britain necessitated the permanent presence of military personnel and administrators. The number of civilian administrative officers was never very great, but by AD 100 there was a very large number of military men in the province. Three legions, probably more than 40 auxiliary cohorts and more than a dozen *alae* (cavalry units) implies a total number in the region of 15,000 legionaries and 30,000 auxiliaries.[1] The Roman presence embraces a huge range of function and status, from the provincial governor down to the ordinary soldier in the ranks, as well as the personnel associated with them, wives and girl-friends, traders, artisans and slaves. We can hardly expect to see the entire array fully represented in our Vindolanda texts, but it is astonishing to find how much of it puts in an appearance, even if only briefly or incidentally. Our texts reveal a great deal of the network of connections between different levels in the hierarchy of function and status and probably touch on almost every element in it. It is equally significant, perhaps, that at this stage in the conquest and absorption of Britannia they completely, or almost completely, exclude the native Britons, as far as we can tell, even though it seems likely that some Celtic-speakers had by this time become thoroughly accustomed to operate in Latin.[2]

At the apex of the hierarchy stood the governor of the province, the *legatus Augusti*, whose authority and appointment derived directly from the emperor under an arrangement which originated in 27 BC when the senate granted to the emperor Augustus a group of the most important provinces with the right to govern them through legates appointed by himself. By AD 100, the governorship of Britain was one of the most senior appointments of this kind and was invariably held by a man of consular rank with proven military and administrative ability. A military diploma of AD 103 shows that at that time the governor of Britain was Lucius Neratius Marcellus and this man is indeed named in one of the texts from Vindolanda. Marcellus was one of a pair of distinguished brothers from Saepinum in Italy (the other, L. Neratius Priscus was a famous jurist) and had held the consulship in AD 95.[3] As we have seen, a draft letter written by Flavius Cerialis at Vindolanda shows the prefect of the Ninth Cohort of Batavians attempting to use influence with someone who might intercede for him with Marcellus, the provincial governor. We do not know what, if anything, Cerialis' letter achieved, but there is some further evidence for the governor's presence and influence in a letter from two fellow-officers to Cerialis wishing him good fortune in his future affairs and referring in somewhat cryptic terms to the prospect of his meeting the governor (presumably Marcellus, though he is not named). We do not know whether there is any relationship between this and Cerialis' draft letter, nor do we know anything about the whereabouts of Marcellus at this time. Given that this was an extremely important period in the history of the Roman occupation of northern Britain, it is overwhelmingly likely that the governor will have spent some time in this region. A visit to Vindolanda itself is not unlikely but there is no direct evidence for this in the tablets.[4] In the letter addressed to Veldedeius, the governor's groom, and found at Vindolanda the presence of the word *Londini*, written on the outside of the leaf, preceding the name of the addressee, suggests a different destination for the letter which might subsequently have been brought back to Vindolanda and dumped.[5]

The provincial governor will surely also have spent time in London and the letter to the groom is one of two scraps of information reflecting a connection between Vindolanda and London. The other is the strength report of the First Cohort of Tungrians which shows that one soldier, probably a centurion, is absent on some duty in London. Such connections are reinforced by the fact that many units, including those stationed at Vindolanda, will have supplied men who were detached for duty with the governor. The Tungrian strength report refers to a group of 46 *singulares legati*, this unit's contribution to a total corps of 500 infantry and 500 cavalry which functioned as the governor's bodyguard and is normally thought to have been based in the Cripplegate fort in London.[6] Access to the governor by letter or petition was surely not confined to the officer class and may be illustrated in a very interesting text on one side of a multiple tablet which contains on the other an account of wheat. This is a draft of a letter or petition written by someone seeking redress for having been unjustly beaten, perhaps by a centurion. The unnamed petitioner mentions that, because he was unable to reach the prefect, he had already approached his *beneficiarius*, but had presumably failed to gain satisfaction. We do not know to whom his present plea was to be directed but in the course of the text he addresses the recipient with the term *maiestas*, which surely can hardly be appropriate to anyone of lower rank than the provincial governor.[7]

These few items of evidence indicate quite clearly the existence of a network through which the provincial governor might be approached. Directly below the governor in the military hierarchy stood the officers of senatorial status, the legionary legates and tribunes who were also part of this network. This small group is apparently not well represented in our Vindolanda material. In the Tungrian strength report, the 46 *singulares legati* are noted as serving in the *officium* of Ferox. We cannot be certain of the identity of Ferox, but it is not unlikely that he was one of the three legionary legates in Britain and he is perhaps most likely to be the legate of the Ninth Legion (Hispana), stationed at York in the 90s. Ferox is identified only by his *cognomen*, but it is an uncommon one, held by only two known men of senatorial rank at this period. Of these, Julius Ferox, who was probably consul in AD 99, is the more likely of the two to have been legate of the Ninth Legion early in the 90s. He is also mentioned by Pliny the Younger in the context of patronage and promotion of the son of a former *primus pilus* (chief centurion) who had gone on to be prefect of an auxiliary cohort. Pliny had known the father as a prefect of a cohort when he himself was a legionary tribune and had tempted him out of retirement to a post on his own staff when he was governor of Bithynia (*c.* AD 110). The son had, as prefect of a cohort, earned the commendation of Julius Ferox, presumably when the latter was holding a senior provincial governorship, and Pliny's letter in turn commends him to the emperor Trajan.[8]

If we had a little more information, we might be able to identify more members of the network of patronage through whom Flavius Cerialis sought to influence the governor Marcellus. The person whom he asks to intercede is named only as Crispinus, an extremely common name which cannot be further identified; but he is quite likely to have been of senatorial rank, in which case he will have been either a legionary legate or a tribune. The physical distance between the senate and the imperial court at Rome and Vindolanda is very great but the evidence of the writing-tablets reveals emphatically that Vindolanda is firmly linked to that relatively small and coherent social and professional world.

The inhabitants of that world are revealed more vividly and in greater detail by consideration of the equestrian officers who figure in the documents and letters, for it is here that the Vindolanda texts come into their own – not surprisingly given the fact that so many of them were discovered in and close to the residence of an equestrian officer.

As a group, the sixty or so equestrian staff officers in command of auxiliary cohorts and cavalry units (*alae*) formed an extremely important element in the military establishment of a heavily garrisoned province like Britain. The equestrian status which such men had meant that they belonged to the census group, defined by a property qualification of at least 400,000 sesterces, second only to the senatorial order. They were thus, by any standards, men of considerable wealth and prestige – at this period the pay of an ordinary legionary soldier was 1200 sesterces (= 300 *denarii*) *per annum*. Their military careers might or might not be spectacular, but they would hold, for an average period of three or four years each, one or more commands (sometimes as many as five or six) of this sort. Most equestrian officers were in their thirties when they obtained their first command and many had had some previous experience, as town magistrates, in municipal administration. But this pattern is by no means universal – there were also some men who were much younger, and some much older (sometimes in their fifties), as well as ex-centurions and sons of centurions. By the beginning of the second century AD, these men were by no means all from Italy – many will have come from provincial towns and the origins of many, if not most, of those serving in Britain are probably in Gaul, Spain and the Alpine regions; people from the province of Gallia Belgica, the most northerly of the three Gallic provinces are likely to be well represented.[9]

In the Vindolanda tablets there are probably about 20 men, writers, addressees, or individuals mentioned in third-person references, who held equestrian commands. Most of them will not have been at Vindolanda. Several are identified by the title *praef(ectus)*, in other cases their status can be inferred with reasonable confidence from the content of a letter or document, or the terms in which they are addressed by another equestrian officer.

It is appropriate to begin with the figure who is central to our documentation – Flavius Cerialis, the prefect of the Ninth Cohort of Batavians, who occupied the *praetorium* at Vindolanda in the years around AD 100. Judged by the criteria specified above, Flavius Cerialis is likely to be an exception to the normal pattern and, as we have seen, for interesting reasons connected with the history of Batavian units serving in the Roman army. Cerialis as a Batavian noble might have commanded his unit for longer than the average three or four years, but we have no other information about his military career. He evidently had a wide range of correspondents among the equestrian officer class, however, and we do know something about at least two of them. Aelius Brocchus was one of Cerialis' most regular correspondents, and it is evident Cerialis and Brocchus and their families were in contact, by corespondence and in person, about social as well as military matters. We do not know where Brocchus was stationed; his wife mentions a place named Briga in one of her letters but the context is too fragmentary for us to be sure that it was their home. Briga, at any rate, is likely to have been near Vindolanda, since one of our accounts almost certainly refers to a visit made there by Cerialis and his family. It requires no elaborate argument to justify identifying Cerialis' correspondent with an equestrian officer named C. Aelius Brocchus who dedicated an inscription in the early second century recording that he held the prestigious command of a cavalry unit, the *ala contariorum*, at the time serving at Arrabona in Pannonia. This posting probably followed his service in Britain.[10] Another officer who turns up on several occasions in Cerialis' correspondence (and perhaps also in a letter to Priscinus) is called Caecilius September; the *cognomen* September is fairly unusual and suggests that Cerialis' correspondent should be identified with one M. Caecilius September, known to have been prefect of a cohort of African Musulamii stationed in Syria in AD 88. One of his letters to Cerialis ends with the phrase *per equitem ad te misi* ('I have sent to you (something [perhaps a letter]) via a cavalryman') and implies that the unit under his command in Britain included cavalry and was therefore either an *ala* or a part-mounted cohort (*cohors equitata*).[11]

There is a limit to what can confidently be deduced from names about their holders' origins. The name Brocchus is common in the east, especially Dalmatia; the occurrence of September in an inscription from Pliny's home town, Comum, in north Italy, may or may not be relevant to Cerialis' fellow-officer. But one text, addressed to a prefect whose name is lost, tempts speculation. The writer, who must also have been a prefect since he describes himself as *col(lega)*, is called Celonius Iustus. The name Celonius is exceedingly rare and does not occur at all in the north-western provinces. But an inscription from Rovenich in Gallia Belgica, now lost, records a certain Celorius Iustus. The name Celorius is not found at all elsewhere and it is quite likely that the name has been miscopied or misread. The reference in his letter to the despatch of a decurion again makes it clear that he was in command of a unit which included cavalry.[12]

Little can said about the others who are known or may be supposed to have been equestrian officers. Julius Verecundus, prefect of the First Cohort of Tungrians, was at Vindolanda, probably early in the 90s. Flavius Genialis and

Priscinus might well also have been in command of units stationed at Vindolanda – the former might have preceded Cerialis as prefect of the Ninth Cohort of Batavians or might have been prefect of the Third, and the latter may well have been in command of the First Cohort of Tungrians after Verecundus. Each of these officers is represented by a small group of letters.[13] Others who are certainly or probably commanders of units tell us little more than their names. Hostilius Flavianus appears to have been at Vindolanda at some point; Vocusius Africanus might have been in command of another Tungrian unit stationed somewhere other than Vindolanda.[14]

The occurrence of the common *gentilicia*, Iulius, Claudius and Flavius, among the officers requires a brief comment. The name Iulius, particularly in the Gallic provinces, often indicates a member of a family whose enfranchisement goes back to the time of Julius Caesar or Augustus. A generation later, the emperor Claudius was particularly generous in granting citizenship in the western provinces and was subjected to a famous and posthumous jibe by Seneca: *constituerat enim omnes Graecos, Gallos, Hispanos, Britannos togatos videre* ('for he had resolved to see all the Greeks, Gauls, Spaniards and Britons wearing the toga').[15] Those turning up with this name in Britain in about AD 100 might be supposed to belong to families enfranchised two generations previously which now saw their members attaining equestrian rank. Those bearing the name Flavius, enfranchised after AD 70, may show swifter success and mobility. We may finally point to one person who was clearly given citizenship in the short reign of the emperor Nerva: M. Cocceius Velox carries that emperor's *gentilicium*, but we do not know anything about his position or rank.[16]

The equestrian officers of the Roman army serving in Britain can be placed in a general context which is comparatively well-known. The Vindolanda tablets offer us a view of another feature of this milieu which is not afforded by any other evidence – the presence and identity of the officers' wives, families and domestic establishments. The historian Tacitus puts into the mouth of Caecina Severus, a conservative traditionalist, a fictional speech in the Roman senate, set in the year AD 21, in which he deplores the growing tendency for senators to take their wives with them to provincial postings:

> inesse mulierum comitatui quae pacem luxu, bellum formidine morentur et Romanum agmen ad similitudinem barbari incessus convertant. non imbecillum tantum et imparem laboribus sexum sed, si licentia adsit, saevum ambitiosum, potestatis avidum; incedere inter milites, habere ad manum centuriones . . .

> An entourage of women involves delays through luxury in peacetime and through panic in war. It turns the Roman army into the likeness of a procession of barbarians. Not only is the female sex weak and unable to bear hardship but, when it has the freedom, it is spiteful, ambitious and greedy for power. They disport themselves among the soldiers and have the centurions eating out of their hands.[17]

This was certainly written in the same period as our texts from Vindolanda but it is perfectly evident that by then it was normal for the equestrian officers to maintain a full family establishment within the *praetorium*. Sulpicia Lepidina, wife of Flavius Cerialis, is the best known of the officers' spouses.[18] Given the comparatively recent enfranchisement of Cerialis' family, it would not be surprising if his wife also came from a recently romanised family. The *gentilicium* suggests that the citizenship may go back to the reign of the emperor Ser. Sulpicius Galba (AD 68–9) but it cannot tell us whether Lepidina herself was the original recipient (and she could, of course, have been somewhat younger than her husband).

Cerialis and Lepidina clearly had children – the footwear found in and near the *praetorium* is sufficient to guarantee the presence of children, and it is possible that at least one of the tablets contains evidence of their writing exercises. Lepidina's most regular correspondent is Claudia Severa, the wife of Aelius Brocchus, and it is clear that she and Lepidina were in the habit of exchanging visits. At the end of her birthday invitation to Lepidina, Severa sent greetings from her husband and her small son (*filiolus*).[19]

The correspondence between Lepidina and Severa was not an isolated phenomenon in the equestrian officer class. Lepidina also received a letter from a woman whose name was probably Paterna. Another letter, perhaps written by a woman named Valatta to Cerialis, refers to some concession made to her through the influence of Lepidina (*per auctoritatem Lepidinae*), doubly interesting for the implication that Cerialis' wife participated in his business even if it was merely social. Thus, the regular inclusion of women in greetings may be somewhat formulaic but need not be considered meaningless: *Pacatam saluta verbis meis* ('greet Pacata in my words') may refer to another wife of an officer, but the name is very common.[20]

The officer's household also included slaves who appear both in the correspondence and the documents. On the back of a letter from Severus to Candidus, referring to some payment for the Saturnalia festival, Candidus is described as a slave of Genialis and there can be no doubt that Severus was also a slave. It is well-known that the Saturnalia in December was a festival of particular significance for slaves – the one day in the year on which they were formally allowed to change places with their owners. Two other letters involve slaves, but the content is very fragmentary in both cases. One is written by Rhenus to Primigenius and Rhenus describes himself as a slave of Similis, that is, presumably Flavius Similis a correspondent of Flavius Corialis. Primigenius is a very common servile name, as is Rhenus in the area of the Rhineland to which the name clearly refers. The other is written by Privatus to Albiso. Albiso is a rare name otherwise attested only for a Christian bishop of the fifth century in Gaul, but Privatus is a common servile name and occurs several times in an account which clearly documents food supplies, some dispensed *per Privatum*, in the *praetorium* over a period of several days. The unnamed writer of the account was probably a slave too, to judge by the note at the end of the account referring to the fact that the '*domini*' have remained at Briga. A letter to Cerialis from a fellow-prefect named Iustinus sends greetings to the *pueri* who are very probably the household slaves. Similarly a letter about various foodstuffs (chickens, eggs, olives and beans) may be addressed to a slave in the household of the prefect Verecundus.[21]

These texts suggest that the organisation of the commander's household was at least partly in the hands of slaves. There were perhaps other slaves connected with the unit at large rather than the *praetorium* in particular but it is impossible to be sure whether or how the distinctions between personal duties in the commander's house and duties elsewhere in the fort were maintained. It may well be that all slaves associated with military personnel were personal property.[22] Be that as it may, one account records transactions through the agency of Gracilis, Audax and Similis, all common servile names. It is tempting, too, though not compelling, to identify some of the holders of Greek names as slaves (or perhaps freedmen): Hermes and Trophimus are two such individuals about whom we have no further information. It need not be supposed that the Greek names necessarily indicate either servile status or an origin in the Greek east, for by this period they were relatively common in all parts of the empire, but there are three more Greek names – Paris, Corinthus and Elpis – which occur in contexts in which the status of the persons is unclear.[23]

About the junior officers, the centurions and decurions, we are rather less well informed, although it is more than likely that this group will have included some people whose rank or position is nowhere stated in our texts. A *beneficiarius* of the prefect, who acted as personal adjutant, turns up as the recipient of supplies of wheat and in a letter of appeal against maltreatment. The presence of a legionary centurion named Annius Equester at Luguvalium (Carlisle), as *centurio regionarius*, provides an important link in the administrative hierarchy as well as a powerful focus of patronage. A centurion of the Third Cohort of Batavians, referred to as the bearer of letters, also has the *cognomen* Equester. Clodius Super, the writer of a letter to Cerialis, is a centurion, perhaps in a legion; the somewhat familiar and non-deferential tone of his letter to the prefect probably indicates that he was of equivalent social standing.[24] Otherwise, the centurions of the auxiliary units at Vindolanda are known in the main simply from references to their centuries and most of the names are too common to tell us anything at all about their holders: Crescens, Felicio, Tullio, Exomnius. A notable oddity is a centurion apparently named Ucenius. This is not otherwise known as a personal name and it may derive from the Alpine tribe of the Ucenni (to be located in Switzerland), one of the subjugated peoples named on the monument which the emperor Augustus erected at La Turbie in the French Alps.[25] Even fewer decurions (officers in charge of *turmae* of cavalry) are known. One, named simply as Lucius, is the recipient of two letters, one mentioning a gift of oysters, the other recording the fact that some cavalrymen had been sent back to their camp on 26 February. Another decurion called Atto (a type of name common in the Gallic and Germanic areas) appeared briefly at Vindolanda on some unspecified mission.[26]

The *principales*, those paid at a higher rate than ordinary soldiers, are equally few. Most interesting is Vittius Adiutor, a standard-bearer (*aquilifer*) of the Second Legion (Augusta), then stationed at Caerleon. Only the beginning of his letter to Cassius Saecularius is preserved but the warm terms in which he addresses him suggest that the two were of similar rank and status (if not actual brothers).[27] Of similar status, too, is a *vexillarius* (flag-bearer) named in an account as Tagamatus or Tagamatius. Names with the prefix Tag- are known in Spain and this man might be associated with a Spanish unit, the First Cohort of Vardulli, since the preceding entry in this account refers to *equites Vardulli*.[28] The occurrence of a *cornicen* (bugler) and of a *duplicarius* with the unusual *gentilicium* Cessaucius is also noteworthy.[29]

The *optiones*, second in command to the centurions and decurions, might be more numerous than our texts explicitly tell us, especially since we know that in general they had a large share of responsibility for the procurement and management of foodstuffs and other supplies with which many of our documents are concerned. The rank is specified on reports which they submitted, in particular the routine reports headed by the word *renuntium*, in which the very common names Candidus and Verecundus occur. One of these was delivered by an *optio* with the fairly unusual name of Arquittius.[30]

There is a certain amount of evidence for soldiers with special duties or particular skills. The governor's groom (*equisio consularis*) Veldeius or Veldedius may be commemorated on a tombstone at Housesteads which bears the name Vilidedius. The form *Veldedeii* occurs on a leather offcut from Vindolanda and the magnificent example of a chamfron found in the excavations (pl. II) may well have belonged to him. This name is clearly of the Celtic type, that of his correspondent Chrauttius seems evidently Germanic, and the mixture is represented in the names of the other members of their circle who are greeted at the end of the letter, Thuttena and Velbuteius. Although we do not know which units they belonged to, their origins must surely be sought in the Rhineland where the Batavian and Tungrian cohorts were originally raised. The social implication of this text is that, at this level as well as that of the equestrian officers, soldiers brought their women with them. Thuttena is described as *soror*, but this need not be taken any more literally than the corresponding common use of the term *frater* between men – she is just as likely to be a female companion of one of the men mentioned.[31]

Other persons with special skills or jobs include a bathman (*balniator*) named Vitalis, a brewer (*cervesarius*) called Atrectus and a shield-maker (*scutarius*) called Lucius. There is also a doctor or medical orderly (*medicus*) called Marcus and two veterinary doctors (*veterinarii*), Virilis and Alio, vital for the care of the horses and other animals associated with military units.[32] The medical personnel will certainly have been serving soldiers but is is more difficult to be certain about the others. If this is true of the *cervesarius* for instance, it has implications for the range of activities performed by military personnel within the fort and its environs. There are many other individuals whom we can see engaged in various transactions which are clearly closely associated with the military establishment at Vindolanda and the fact that many of them are mentioned in letters and documents found in the *praetorium* area must be significant. We have a letter from Metto to Advectus mainly concerning the transport of component parts of vehicles through an intermediary named Saco. On three occasions we meet Gavo, a supplier of clothing (another unattested name, though the cognate *Gauva* does occur once in Gallia Belgica). The subject of the letter of recommendation is called Brigionus, a name which is clearly of Celtic origin, modified by the addition of a Latin suffix.[33] From the barrack-block in Period 4 we have a small but important group of texts in which various individual names recur. These record the financial transactions of Octavius and Candidus in the procurement and transportation of various commodities, and the dispensation of wheat to military personnel including legionary soldiers (and also, apparently, to the father of the writer of the account). These texts mention other individuals with recognisably Roman names: Firmus, Spectatus, Frontius, Frontinius Iulius, Macrinus, Marinus, Felicius Victor, Crescens, Amabilis and so on.[34] The adoption of Roman names by auxiliary soldiers is a very well-known phenomenon, as is vividly shown by a letter on a papyrus from Egypt, written by a recent recruit to the fleet named Apion to his father Epimachus: 'my name is Antonius Maximus, my century the Athenonica'.[35] Of all the names which occur in this group of texts, the most frequent is Candidus and, although it is tempting to place him at the centre of the group for that reason, the name is so common that we cannot attach much significance to any possible identification. Elsewhere in the Vindolanda texts and from earlier periods we have at least two men called Candidus, one a slave of the officer Genialis, and the other an *optio*. If the Candidus from the texts of the barrack-block is either of these, he is more likely to be the latter and it is perhaps not out of the question that an *optio* might have served at the same fort for an extended period of time.[36]

This evidence all contributes to our understanding of the nature of the mix in the community at Vindolanda. Given that we know of the involvement of centurions and *optiones* in transactions of the sort recorded in these texts, it might be reasonable to suppose that this is the milieu from which these texts come. In taking a view of the whole period which the texts cover, however, it might be safer to suppose that below the level of the commanding officers we are dealing with a wide range of people, including junior officers, slaves and probably civilians as well. Firm identification of the latter in connection with the Roman army has always proved problematical and the lack of evidence in Britain for the presence of a mercantile class supporting and profiting from the presence of the army has been noted. It is noteworthy that the person who wrote the draft petition on the back of the wheat account describes himself as *homo trasmarinus* (a man from overseas) and writes about his maltreatment in terms which suggests beyond reasonable doubt that he is a civilian who has suffered at the hands of the military. It may be, therefore, that Vindolanda now supplies some evidence for the civilian presence.[37] If so, it is overwhelmingly likely that in the frontier region at this date all such people were, like the writer of the petition, men from abroad rather than native Britons. The development of commerce and urbanisation in the Rhineland, and particularly in the Batavian area, was sufficient to provide the foundation for the growth of such a mercantile class.[38]

We come finally to consider the ordinary soldiers at Vindolanda. Here we are naturally driven to be more reliant on guesswork since it is inevitable that the lower ranks should be less heavily represented in written material and more likely than not that, when and if they do appear, their names will not be qualified by description or rank. It was inferred, for instance, that the persons in the very first of the Vindolanda tablets to come to light, a letter referring to the despatch of clothing, had names which suggested the milieu of the ordinary soldier: Tetricus, Elpis, Sattua.[39] But it must be admitted that such a judgement is largely intuitive and cannot be proved.

When we come to examples of which we can be more certain, we normally have nothing but a bare, uninformative and often very common name to go on, for example, Fuscus, Expeditus, Albinus, Festus.[40] We can, however, sometimes do better. One of our accounts contains the very common name Sabinus, but he is distinguished by the addition of his place of origin, *Trever* (from Trier), which fits perfectly with membership of a Tungrian or Batavian unit. The requests for leave (*commeatus*) might be presumed to come from ordinary soldiers and we should note one reasonably common name, Buccus, and another, Messicus, attested only once.[41]

Otherwise, our lists and accounts offer examples of names of Celtic, Germanic, Spanish or Balkan origin, which probably represent the ordinary soldiery of the units. Some are common, like Tetricus and Sanctus, others are infrequent or previously unattested. For example: Acranius is previously unknown; Andecarus is a fairly common Gaulish name; a name beginning Andle– might be related to the name of a Spanish deity called Andlis; Gambax is unattested but might be compared with Gamburio (Gallia Belgica), or Gamba (Salona); Ircucisso, if correctly read, looks odd, but there is an Irducissa in Pannonia; Sautenus evokes comparison with Sautus and Sautenius which occur in Gallia Belgica; Vattus looks as if it might be common but turns up only in Italy; Butimas is unattested but Boutius is common in Spain, Butes occurs in Dacia, and Bouti in London and Dalmatia.[42]

None of this will take us very far with the individual lives, careers or concerns of the ordinary soldiers at Vindolanda, to be sure, and we can envisage on their part only limited participation in the literate world (cf. Chapter 7). What little we can deduce, however, reminds us that the social and geographical range from which the inhabitants came was quite broad and diverse. What unites them is membership of or links with the Roman military establishment in a region in which they were all foreigners. At least in the world of Vindolanda their presence makes more impression, as far as we can tell, than that of the native *Brittunculi*.

NOTES

1 For the Roman army of Britain see Holder (1982).

2 Richmond (1953).

3 For the governors of Britain see A. R. Birley (1981) and for Neratius Marcellus id. 87–91 and (1991), 95–100.

4 Cf. A. R. Birley (1991), 89.

5 **28**. For the explanation of place-names in the addresses on the outside of letters see *Tab. Vindol.* II, pp. 43–5.

6 **1**.5–6, 9. For the *singulares* see M. P. Speidel (1978), Appendix I, 126–9, Hassall (1973), 231–7.

7 **33**.

8 **1**.5–6 note, Pliny, *Ep.* 10.87.

9 In most cases there is no explicit evidence for the origins of officers. This notion is based on the fact that Batavian units were commanded by their own nobles (see p. 26) and by the occurrence of names which are peculiar to or common in the area of Gallia Belgica (these are listed for the individual provinces in *NPEL*).

10 Brocchus, *Tab. Vindol.* II 233, 243–8, *CIL* 3.4360, cf. *VRR* II, 38–9. Briga, **22**.c.v.2.

11 *Tab. Vindol.* II 234, 252–3. Letter to Priscinus(?), *Tab. Vindol.* II 298. See *PME* I C26, cf. A. R. Birley (1991), 98–9.

12 *Tab. Vindol.* II 345, *CIL* 13.7937, cf. *VRR* II, 31.

13 Verecundus, *Tab. Vindol.* II 210–12. Genialis, *Tab. Vindol.* II 217–24. Priscinus, *Tab. Vindol.* II 295–8.

14 Flavianus, *Tab. Vindol.* II 261, cf. 172. Africanus, *Tab. Vindol.* II 315. Others whose names or correspondence suggest that they might have been prefects include: Oppius Niger (**23**), Claudius Karus (**19**), Flavius Similis (*Tab. Vindol.* II 358, 281, 444), Iustinus (260), Veranius (319), Licinius Asper (224), Vettius Severus (305), Pastor (259), Valerius Niger (465), Flavius Proculus (219), Flavius Conianus (296).

15 Seneca, *Apocolocyntosis* 3.3.

16 *Tab. Vindol.* II 352.

17 Tacitus, *Ann.* 3.33.

18 **21–2**, *Tab. Vindol.* II 293–4. For women in this context see Allason-Jones (1989), chs 2, 4.

19 Footwear, *VRR* III, 45–6. Writing-exercise (?), *Tab. Vindol.* II 118. Birthday invitation, **21**.ii.9–10. The alternative reading and interpretation suggested by A. R. Birley (1991), 101 (cf. *VRR* II, 39) is not persuasive, see *Tab. Vindol.* II 291.ii.9–10 note.

20 *Tab. Vindol.* II 294, 257, 353.

21 Severus to Candidus, **25**. Rhenus to Primigenius, *Tab. Vindol.* II 347. Privatus to Albiso, *Tab. Vindol.* II 303. *per Privatum* etc., **10**.26, 28, 31, 35, 38. Iustinus, *Tab. Vindol.* II 260. Foodstuffs, **26**.

22 M. P. Speidel (1989).

23 Gracilis etc., **186**. Hermes, *Tab. Vindol.* II 487. Trophimus, *Tab. Vindol.* II 341. Paris and Corinthus, **29**. Elpis, **34**.

24 On the career structure of junior officers in auxiliary units, for which there is not much evidence, see Breeze (1974), 278–86. *beneficiarius*, **6**.18, **33**.i.10. *centurio regionarius*, **19**. Centurion of the Third Cohort, *Tab. Vindol.* II 263. Clodius Super, **20**.

25 Crescens, *Tab. Vindol.* II 128. Felicio, *Tab. Vindol.* II 138, 166, 168, **8**.i.6. Tullio, **9**.iii.31. Exomnius, **8**.ii.13. Ucenius (?), **9**.i.1. Augustan monument, Pliny, *Natural History* 3.137, *EJ*² 40.

26 Lucius, **24**, *Tab. Vindol.* II 300. Atto, *Tab. Vindol.* II 345.

27 *Tab. Vindol.* II 214. This is based on a reading and interpretation different from that proposed by A. R. Birley (1990b).

28 Sollemnis to Paris, **29**. *vexillarius*, **7**.15. For the cohort of Vardulli see *CIL* 16.43 (cf. *VRR* II, 5).

29 *cornicen*, **8**.i.1. *duplicarius*, **30**.back 2–3.

30 Foodstuffs and supplies, note particularly **6** and **32**. Reports with *renuntium* heading, **4**, *Tab. Vindol.* II 127–53. Arquittius, *Tab. Vindol.* II 128.

31 **28**. Tombstone *RIB* 1420. Offcut, *VRR* II, 94, no.12.

32 *balniator*, **7**.8. *cervesarius*, **8**.ii.14. *scutarius*, **9**.ii.21. *medicus*, *Tab. Vindol.* II 156.2. *veterinarii*, **7**.7, **28**.i.10–2.

33 Metto to Advectus, **27**. Gavo, **12**, *Tab. Vindol.* II 207, 218.3. Gauua, *CIL* 13.3409. Brigionus, **19**.i.3; the name Brigio in *Tab. Vindol.* II 188.10 may refer to the same person.

34 **6**, **7**, **8**, **32**, **33**.

35 *BGU* II 423 = *SP* I 112.

36 Slave, **25**. *optio*, *Tab. Vindol.* II 146, 148.

37 Petition, **33**. For the lack of clear evidence for civilians see Breeze (1984), 58–9.

38 See Bloemers (1983), 168–70.

39 **34**.

40 *Tab. Vindol.* II 161.

41 Sabinus, **8**.i.4. Buccus, *Tab. Vindol.* II 176.1. Messicus, **5** β.3.

42 Tetricus, **34**.ii.3. Sanctus, **8**.ii.18. Acranius, **7**.12. Andecarus, **8**.ii.17. Gambax, **9**.i.5. Ircucisso, **8**.i.5, Sautenus, *Tab. Vindol.* II 182.back.i5. Vattus, **8**.ii.10. Butimas, **9**.iii.35. Notes and relevant references for all these names can be found in the commentaries to the individual texts in *Tab. Vindol.* II.

6

SOCIAL AND ECONOMIC LIFE ON THE FRONTIER

LIFE IN THE *PRAETORIUM*

Amongst the writing-tablets discovered in the 1987 season was a group of four small and unprepossessing fragments which belong together. The text which can be more or less reconstructed offers us what is evidently a list or inventory, whose nature and significance has to be deduced entirely from its content, a familiar characteristic of the Vindolanda documents. In the list we have first *scutulae* (dishes or plates), then *paropsides* (side-plates), *acetabula* (vinegar-bowls), *ovaria* (egg-cups); after that, perhaps stored on a cross-beam or purlin, a *lanx* (a platter), more *scutulae*, then a *compendiarium* (perhaps meaning a strong-box), a *lucerna* (lamp) made of bronze, some *panaria* (bread-baskets), *calices* (cups) and some *trullae* (bowls of another type) *in theca* (in a chest). The numerals referring to the individual items are not completely preserved but it seems clear that there were no more than a few of each of these utensils and it is also obvious that the document is not complete. A first assessment might put this into the 'laundry-list category', a trivial item which is not likely to tell us very much, although many of these items can be archaeologically documented at Vindolanda and elsewhere.[1]

Such lists of household objects are not uncommon in the Greek papyri from Egypt and the word *ovaria*, which is at first sight difficult to parallel with this meaning, in fact exists in a Greek transliteration. A search for parallels soon discloses a helpful Greek text from Egypt which probably dates to around AD 50 and offers an insight into a much grander lifestyle; despite being incomplete it contains inventories of 3 sets of silver tableware, of which the second, in a chest inscribed with the name of Gallus, enumerates 54 vinegar-bowls, 2 sauceboats, 12 mushroom dishes, 24 plates, 26 dish-rests, 20 egg-cups, 2 large plates in cases, another very large plate, an altar, a saucer, 2 serving spoons and 15 small spoons. The total weight of the silver is more than 310 Roman lbs (*librae*) and its value will therefore be over 25,000 *denarii* or 100,000 sesterces, about a quarter of the total property qualification required for membership of the Roman equestrian class. The Gallus who owned this dinner service must have been a very wealthy man, and it is tempting to wonder whether this might actually be an official list of part of the property of the first ill-starred prefect of Egypt, Cornelius Gallus, which was confiscated by the emperor Augustus in 27 or 26 BC and was perhaps still preserved intact several decades after Gallus' demise.[2] Be that as it may, our Vindolanda inventory is clearly comparable in type and although it takes us into a less wealthy milieu (there is no indication that any of these items were made of silver), it is worth remembering that the cohort commanders at Vindolanda were of equestrian status and thus belonged to the same social and property class as Cornelius Gallus.

The Vindolanda list bears every indication of including the dinner service and other domestic utensils which must have belonged to the household of the commanding officer in the *praetorium*, and the archaeological context of this writing-tablet places it in a room which has been identified as the kitchen during the period when the building was occupied by Flavius Cerialis and his wife Sulpicia Lepidina.[3] These may have been their personal possessions or, if this was all army property, the inventory may have been prepared for them by their predecessors or by them for their successors. It provides an invaluable clue to the nature and import of the significant number of texts which enable us to illustrate many features of social and economic life at Vindolanda in this period.

The chronological divisions and the physical development of the site allow us to focus on the lives of the inhabitants of the *praetorium* for the earlier part of the period (*c.* AD 92–103) and on the occupants of the barrack-block and the workshop thereafter. The picture will be admittedly partial and fragmentary, but for Britain, and especially northern Britain, it is unique in its detail and coherence. It hardly needs to be emphasised that our evidence for the bric-à-brac of social history in the Roman empire derives largely from literary sources which do not directly reflect the details of life in the garrison posts on northern frontiers. It is therefore fascinating to observe the extent to which our evidence for lifestyle on the frontiers does echo the world evoked by contemporary literary sources for social history. We then move on to consider the evidence which might be relevant beyond the confines of the *praetorium* and the broader implications of the Vindolanda tablets for the economic and social development of northern Britain at this period.

Central to our picture, then, is the period of a few years around AD 100 when the *praetorium* was occupied by Flavius Cerialis, the prefect of the Ninth Cohort of Batavians, a position which he is likely to have held, by analogy with the known lengths of tenure of equestrian officer posts in the Roman army, for at least three or four years.[4] Since the nature and organisation of the commander's establishment in the *praetorium* in the preceding period are likely to have been very similar, although the building was of rather poorer quality, the picture can legitimately be treated, to a certain extent, synchronically.[5] Even if we cannot be sure that all of the domestic accounts reflect the occupation of Cerialis, we can be confident that things will not have been much different a decade before or after his posting at Vindolanda. The domestic organisation in the *praetorium* was clearly quite highly developed and it might at first be thought surprising that such detailed written records were kept at all. There is no doubt, however, that it fits very well into the context of the well-to-do Roman *familia* – the most surprising feature may turn out to be the fact that the inhabitants are romanised Batavian élites.[6]

It is worth pausing for a moment to consider the organisation of the commander's household in a little more detail. An account of foodstuffs which has already been discussed certainly involves at least two slaves, the unnamed writer and Privatus, through whom some transactions are performed.[7] From this it is but a short and entirely justifiable step to the supposition that much of the organisational and accounting work in the *praetorium* will have been done by the slaves, some of whom were identified in Chapter 5. This role at once invites comparison with the well-known phenomenon – both in fiction and reality – of the efficient and literate domestic slaves in the upper-class Roman *familia*, from the imperial household down. Perhaps it is not particularly surprising, then, to find that it is also a feature of the lifestyle of the equestrian army officers, but it should be emphasised that, once again, the evidence which Vindolanda provides for it is unique. The existence of slaves in the military context is known – they seem to have functioned as personal attendants, grooms or batmen to the soldiers, but we have found no clear evidence of slaves performing these functions at Vindolanda. There are also records on papyri of soldiers buying and selling slaves. Two of the slaves at Vindolanda, Candidus and Rhenus, are designated as belonging to individual officers, Genialis and Similis respectively, and there may be a third, whose name is lost, belonging to Verecundus. A correspondent of Cerialis who is a centurion makes reference to clothing needed for his *pueri* which almost certainly means slaves.[8] This must mean that they were the personal property of the officers concerned, rather than belonging to the unit at large. One fragmentary text, which seems to be a petition or complaint about the theft of a belt, might well imply that a separate bathing-establishment was maintained for slaves and this would be in keeping with Roman social distinctions.[9] It is probable that this applies to the other slaves as well. Whether they had any role to play outside the *praetorium* is not clear, but we cannot, of course, divorce their activities within it from the general military context of the fort.

It is the records of food, clothing and domestic equipment which contribute most to our picture of the standard of living in an officer's residence. Some of the accounts of food show detailed record-keeping of individual items on a daily basis. One of the longest accounts, which had earlier been identified as an official document but must clearly relate to the *praetorium*, contains an itemised daily record over a period of several days in June and records mainly *hordeum* (barley) and *cervesa* (Celtic beer). A greater variety of foodstuffs is listed for one particular day, including *vinum* (vintage-wine), *acetum* (sour wine) and *muria* (fish-sauce). The comparatively large quantity of barley may be a sign of the presence of animals or it may be used as a substitute for *frumentum* (wheat). The absence of the latter from this account is striking but it may simply be due to the fact that this is not a record of regular soldiers' rations or staple items but of supplies for the commander's household. It certainly reflects a much wider range of foodstuffs than the basic military diet possibly including, if it is correctly read and interpreted, a reference to Massic wine, a high-class luxury imported from Italy.[10] The same general impression is conveyed by a shorter account which records purchases of meat for cash, including *perna* (ham), *porcellum* (pork), *caprea* (roe-deer) and *cervina* (venison), as well as *condimenta* (spices), *sal* (salt), *bracis* (a cereal which was used for malting amongst other things) and *frumentum* (wheat). This account twice has a notation which might indicate that the items were for use *in praetorio* and the amount and variety of meat would certainly fit the supposition that this quality and range of diet is more likely to be found in the *praetorium* than the barracks. It is particularly interesting that, despite the plentiful archaeological evidence for the presence of sheep, mutton or lamb nowhere appears in our food lists; this may well be due to the predominance of pork and beef in the Gallic taste.[11] This account, like many others, indicates cash payments for some of the items and alerts us to the fact that we are not simply in the presence of a system supply by requisition, but a more flexible and sophisticated 'local economy', an impression which will be consistently reinforced in the following pages.

LIST OF FOODSTUFFS[12]

Acetum	Sour wine	**10**, 202
Alium(?)	Garlic	233
Alliatum	Garlic paste	208
Amulum(?)	Meal	204
Apua	Small fish	271
Avena	Fodder	185
Axungia	Pork-fat	**8**, **10**
Bracis	Cereal	**11**, **32**, 348
Buturum(?)	Butter	204
Callum	Pork-crackling	233
Caprea	Roe-deer	**11**
Cervesa	Beer	**10**, 186
Cervina	Venison	**11**
Condimenta	Spices	**11**, 193
Conditum	Pickling liquor	208
Fabae	Beans	**12**, **26**
Faex(?)	Lees of wine	185
Frumentum	Wheat	**6**, **11**, 185
(H)alica	Semolina	193, 233
(Caro) hircina(?)	Goat-meat	186
Hordeum	Barley	**10**, 213, 185
Lardum	Lard	**8**
Lens(?)	Lentil	204
Ligusticum(?)	Lovage	204
Malum	Apple	**26**
Mel	Honey	**12**
Mulsum	Wine and honey	**26**
Muria	Fish-sauce	**10**, **26**, 202
Offella	Pork cutlet	203
Oleum	Oil	203
Olivae	Olives	**26**
Ostria	Oysters	**24**
Ova	Eggs	**26**, 193
Panis	Bread	**6**, 203
Perna	Ham	**8**, **11**

Piper	Pepper	**9**
Porcellum	Young pig	**11**
Prunolum(?)	Plum	**189**
Pullus	Chicken	**26**
Radices	Radishes	**25**
Sal	Salt	**11**, 185, 186
Spica	Cereal	**32**
Turta	Twisted loaf	**6**
Vinum	Wine	**10**, 203
Ungella	Pig's trotter	233

The table lists the range of foodstuffs which appear in the tablets and suggests a high degree of sophistication and variety in diet. Many of the texts in which these items occur are likely to be relevant to the *praetorium* in Periods 2 and 3. One of the accounts of Gavo includes quantities of beans and honey purchased. Another brief list, annotated at the left with the letters *rec*, perhaps an abbreviation for *receptum*, contains *condimenta* (spices), *halica* (semolina) and *ova* (eggs), perhaps supplied on loan to a certain Felicio. The writers of letters sometimes refer to purchases of foodstuffs and incidentally cast an interesting light on the operation of price variations in the local markets. A letter to Candidus, the slave of Genialis, mentions the purchase of radishes to the value of not less than half a *denarius*. In a more explicit example, the writer of a letter perhaps addressed to a slave of the prefect Verecundus, refers to the purchase of 20 chickens and seems to be instructing his correspondent to buy good-looking apples (*mala formonsa*) and eggs in large quantities *si ibi aequo emantur* ('if they are on sale there at a fair price'). The references to a *modius* of olives – obviously imported – and 2 *modii* of ground beans (*fabae frensae*) in this text is also of considerable interest. The occurrence of the word *mulsum*, a drink made of wine and honey, in a fragmentary context which may also refer to inebriation, suggests a due regard for the pleasures of life. The letter neatly undermines any notion of an economy dominated by primitive methods of barter in undeveloped frontier regions and also suggests that the needs of military personnel were not simply met by an official system of requisition or compulsory purchase; this may well have applied to official rations, of course. Whether all this betokens the practice of *haute cuisine* in the *praetorium* is another matter. A copy or draft of a letter from Cerialis to Brocchus on a leaf which was re-used contains a list of three culinary items, pig's trotters, and probably pork-crackling and semolina, and it is perhaps not beyond the realms of possibility that we also have a fragment of a recipe from Lepidina's kitchen in one text which has references to a *scutula* (small dish), possibly a *poculum* (cup) and perhaps the phrase *in lance* (on a tray or plate).[13] This tablet was actually found in the kitchen of the Period 3 *praetorium*, along with the inventory, discussed at the beginning of this chapter which shows clearly that the household had a proper stock of utensils.

There is also good evidence for the supply of clothing at Vindolanda. The accounts of Gavo suggest that he played an important role in this aspect of supply. One text, which might concern personnel in the unit rather than the officers, twice records tunics as having been obtained from a named person, in one case Brocchus, presumably the officer Aelius Brocchus, and in another an unknown person called Tranquillus. The letter to Cerialis from Clodius Super, a centurion, asks him to send 6 *sagaciae*, 7 *palliola* and 6 *tunicae* for Super's *pueri*, by which he almost certainly means his slaves. Cerialis himself wrote a letter in which he envisaged purchasing something, perhaps clothing, to give him protection against the winter weather. That such transactions were routine is clearly indicated by a fragment of an account which records repayment of loan, another which may refer to the purchase of clothing, amongst other items, in the course of a journey and a letter mentioning the purchase of, and accounting for, some items at a price of 3 *victoriati* each, the *victoriatus* being a coin worth half a *denarius*. The use of small change was clearly ubiquitous.[14]

We can be sure that the equestrian officers and their families were as well clothed as they were nourished since a small number of documents, similar in kind to the inventory of kitchenware and found in close proximity, provides us with a unique glimpse of range and type of garments to be found in the *praetorium*. Here we may have the inventory of the upper-crust military wardrobes, and we must surely suppose that, even if the utensils were army property, the clothing was the personal property of the family. The lists include *calcei* (shoes), *galliculae* (a diminutive of *gallica*, a Gallic type of shoe or sandal), perhaps some footwear qualified by the adjective *balnearia* (for use in the baths), *subuclae* (vests, elewhere called *subunculae*), *subpaenula* (a lexical curiosity evidently indicating something worn beneath the *paenula*), *tunicae*, *tunicae cenatoriae* (tunics of fine wool fabric with woven decoration), *cubitoria* (a collective word for a dinner ensemble), *abolla* (a thick, heavy cloak, perhaps an *abolla cenatoria*). For some of these items we have the heading *de synthesi*, a collective word for a costume of separable but matching elements. Some of these items will no doubt have been brought by the family when they came to Vindolanda, but it is clear from these and other texts that there was a steady flow of supply, perhaps in two directions. These lists also contain *lodices* (blankets) and perhaps *cervicalia* (cushions). One of the two accounts of Gavo, lists *saga* (cloaks), *tosseae* (some kind of rug, referred to in a famous third-century inscription from Thorigny as *tosseae Britannicae*) and a *bedox* (bedspread or something similar). This list also records a quantity of wool (*lana*), which suggests that there may well have been some manufacture at the site – there is ample evidence for the presence of sheep at Vindolanda and it is probable that local manufacture was able to supply all or most of the needs of the Roman army of Britain.[15] All the textiles with tapestry-woven ornament come from a Room (x) in the Period 3 *praetorium* and probably therefore belonged to the wardrobe of Cerialis and Lepidina. So clearly, did some of the footwear (of which there is a huge quantity), including some high-class products and shoes worn by women and children. The importance of the evidence for clothing is that it gives us a group of terms of known context and date (although some like *subpaenula* are strikingly new) and an idea of the range of clothing available on the northern frontier at this time. It is striking that in general it is in keeping with the society much closer to the heart of the empire which is revealed by contemporary literary sources such as Martial and Juvenal.[16]

The small finds and artefacts from Vindolanda give us a much more vivid impression than do the texts of the material possessions of the inhabitants, and it is worth noting that one of our texts refers to items of jewellery in the shape of *anuli* (rings), probably set with precious or semi-precious stones.[17]

It is, of course, not surprising to find that the officers and soldiers in the Roman army were well-fed, well-clothed, and able to procure a wide range of goods. What the evidence underlines, again, is the sophistication of the level and methods of demand and supply at this time, in this region and amongst these troops from northern Europe. The limited opportunities we have to compare our evidence with that of the papyri from Egypt, for example, reveal striking similarities with an area which had a much longer tradition of monetisation, trade and commerce. Another simple comparison adds emphasis. A list of the items of food and clothing at Vindolanda set against the comprehensive catalogues of goods provided in the Maximum Price Edict of Diocletian (issued in AD 301) assures us the people at Vindolanda availed themselves of a high proportion of the range of goods available in the Roman world to those who could afford them.[18] We will, of course, want to know how far the picture of an officer's life at Vindolanda compares in detail with what we know of other places at this period. The answer is simple. Papyri and ostraka from Egypt provide some comparable evidence. A soldier named Terentianus, stationed in Arabia at the beginning of the second century AD, wrote letters to his family in the Egyptian village of Karanis, referring in detail to a a large number of personal possessions and material requirements. There are similar letters on ostraka from an oasis site and from Mons Claudianus in the eastern desert.[19] But there is no comparable amount of coherent, detailed evidence from any single site, especially not in Roman Britain. Vindolanda and its writing-tablets are unique.

The tablets also give us some opportunity to observe the social habits and preoccupations which this lifestyle entailed and supported. Amongst activities outside the daily routine celebrations of various kinds loom quite large and several have interesting religious connections. The account of foodstuffs which we have already discussed lists small cash payments *ad sacrum*, which must be for some religious or ceremonial purpose. It is notable that the date for which a larger than normal range of foodstuffs is listed in eight separate entries, 24 June, was an important one in the Roman religious calendar, the festival of the goddess Fors Fortuna, a particularly popular deity in the army. One of the items recorded for this date, *axungia* (pork-fat) is credited to the commander for charitable donations (*stipes*), perhaps as a loan, and some of the wine is also for religious uses, *ad sacrum d<i>vae*. There is also evidence for a religious observance on another occasion in a letter to Flavius Cerialis which begins: *ego frater sacrificio diem Kalendarum sicut volueras dedi[caui* ('just as you wished, brother, I have consecrated the day of the Kalends by a sacrifice'). The *dies Kalendarum* is New Year's Day and was celebrated all over the Roman world. One of the more intriguing letters to Cerialis, from a correspondent named Hostilius Flavianus, begins with a New Year's greeting – *annum novom faustum felicem* ('a happy and prosperous New Year'); it is possible that the writer of the first letter, whose name is lost, was also Hostilius Flavianus. Few though these items are, they underline the institutionalisation of religion in the Roman army and recall the great calendar of religious festivals preserved in a famous papyrus from Doura-Europos; just as the latter gives no sign of any cultural or religious influence of the local cults of the unit at Doura (the Twentieth Cohort of Palmyrene Archers), so the evidence from Vindolanda reveals nothing characteristically Batavian or Gallic.[20]

A letter from Severus to Candidus reveals evidence for a religious occasion of a rather different kind within the household, the Saturnalia which was celebrated at the end of December (and therefore certainly influenced the timing of the later

Christian festival associated with that period of the year). This brief note is difficult to interpret and it is especially irritating that it has not proved possible to specify the nature of the item which is the subject of a payment and is qualified by the adjective *saturnalicium*. It is, however, interesting that the address on the back of the letter reveals that Candidus is a slave of Genialis, an officer perhaps resident at Vindolanda in Period 2, and his correspondent Severus was also a slave. The Saturnalia was of particular significance for slaves since it was the one day in the year on which they could change roles with their owners and enjoy the privilege of being waited on.[21]

These religious observances are all situated within the context of the *praetorium*. We have virtually no information about the broader context, but it is worth noting that the wheat account which we have already discussed includes a dispensation to someone *ad fanum* (at the shrine), which may be an elliptical reference to a local site.[22] Given the importance of religious observances in the army, facilities of this nature may have been almost as routine as hospitals and bath-houses. Such activity is probably reflected in a fragmentary letter with a reference to a *sacerdos* (priest) and perhaps a festival.[23]

The officer's household gives us more explicit evidence for celebration of a different kind in one of the most striking of all the letters from Vindolanda. Claudia Severa, the wife of Aelius Brocchus, writes to Sulpicia Lepidina inviting her to a birthday party on 11 September: *iii idus Septembres soror ad diem sollemnem natalem meum rogo libenter facias ut venias ad nos iucundiorem mihi diem interventu tuo factura* . . . ('on 11 September, sister, for the day of the celebration of my birthday, I give you a warm invitation to make sure that you come to us, to make the day more enjoyable for me by your arrival . . .'). There is another curious reference to a birthday in a fragmentary draft or copy of a letter written by the hand which we have identified as that of Cerialis himself. In the phrase *natalem Cerialis mei* ('the birthday of my Cerialis'), the first word has been erased and *valetudinem* (meaning health, perhaps ill-health) has been written above. This may be Cerialis writing at Lepidina's dictation a letter in which she at first wished to draw attention to her husband's birthday, but then felt compelled to make an excuse involving illness. Alternatively, if this is Cerialis writing his own letter, it may be that the Cerialis named is a son. Lepidina too may have been troubled by illness; one of her correspondents seems to be promising to bring her some medicine for a fever.[24]

We do not know whether Lepidina went to Severa's party but it is not unlikely. The end of the account of foodstuffs from Cerialis' period in the *praetorium* carries the annotation *domini Brigae manserunt* ('the lords have remained at Briga), presumably written by a slave of the household and referring to the officer and his family and show that the family must have visited Briga on at least one occasion. Another letter to Lepidina indicates that this is a place where Claudia Severa was intending to stay. In this letter Severa says that she has asked Brocchus' permission to make a visit to Lepidina: *sicut tecum locuta fueram et promiseram ut peterem a Broccho et venirem at te; peti et respondit mihi ita corde semper licitum . . . quomodocumque possim at te pervenire* ('just as I had spoken with you and promised that I would ask Brocchus and would come to you, I asked him and he gave me the following reply, that it was always readily permitted to me, together with . . . to come to you in whatever way I can'). Later in the letter Severa indicates that she will stay at Briga in the phrase *et Brigae mansura*. One way to interpret this is that the conversation which Severa mentions took place on the occasion of Lepidina's visit to Briga for the birthday party and that Severa is now planning a return visit to Lepidina at Vindolanda. It is equally possible, however, that the explicit reference to a stay at Briga indicates that this is *not* Severa's home base. It is most unfortunate that we cannot identify Briga – the word is a common Celtic place-name element meaning 'hill'; the one place in Britain previously known to have it is in the south and certainly too far away to be relevant to the text from Vindolanda. The period around AD 100 is too early to permit identification with Stanwix but an inscription found nearby refers to a '*civitas Bricic*' and would connect it with the Brigantes.[25]

The officers themselves perhaps also had time for leisure activities during such exchanges of visits. In one of his letters to Brocchus Cerialis begins: *si me amas, frater, rogo mittas mihi plagas* ('if you love me brother, I ask that you send me some hunting-nets'); hunting was certainly an officer's sport in this region. A third-century re-dedication of an altar to the deity Silvanus, found near Stanhope in Weardale, records the activities of an equestrian officer, perhaps visiting from Lancaster: *C. Tetius Veturius Micianus pr[(a)e]f(ectus) alae Sebosiannae ob aprum eximiae formae captum quem multi antecessores eius praedari non potuerunt v(oto) s(uscepto) l(ibens) p(osuit)* ('Gaius Tetius Veturius Micianus, prefect of the Sebosian cavalry regiment, on fulfilment of his vow willingly set up this for taking a wild boar of remarkable fineness which many of his predecessors had been unable to bag'). A relief found at Housesteads, very close to Vindolanda, vividly illustrates a stag confronted by the hunter's net.[26]

These texts give us a remarkable insight into the sophistication of the lifestyle and the degree of social and economic cohesion achieved by the officer class in the frontier region. Although the contacts between Cerialis/Lepidina and Brocchus/Severa are the most vividly attested, the number of other officers attested in Cerialis' correspondence assures us that the range of contact was broad, and although many of these individuals probably shared a common ethnic background there is no reason to assume that they all did so. Severa was Lepidina's most frequent correspondent, but there is one other, Paterna, who writes to Lepidina in warm terms; another woman named Valatta writes to Cerialis referring to an intercession made by Lepidina on her behalf. Although there is little explicit evidence for children in our documents, we are forcibly reminded of the wider definition and coherence of the Roman *familia* by the slaves and the way in which their behaviour reflects that of the *domini*.[27]

LIFE IN THE RANKS

The evidence which takes us outside the immediate context of the *praetorium*, comes from the later periods of the barracks and the workshop and may reflect the lives of the senior NCOs, the centurions and *optiones*, rather than the ordinary soldiers. But the long account which records the dispensation of over 300 *modii* of *frumentum* (wheat) to various individuals includes a group of legionary soldiers. Though wheat was, of course, a staple item and part of the standard issue of rations to soldiers, the relationship between such a standard issue and this distribution is not made clear in our text. But one entry records that the wheat given to Lucco is for personal use (*in ussus suos*), another records a loan, others suggest that it is being used for baking bread and twisted loaves (*turtas*). The inference that baking is done on site is hardly surprising and in peacetime soldiers would normally expect to eat fresh bread.[28] Another account which records a fairly large quantity of lard (*lardum*). Livestock was clearly kept under military supervision and the notion that Roman soldiers did not eat meat cannot be sustained; it is difficult to tell from the tablets just how much meat was consumed outside the officer class, however. Similarly, although wine was clearly available, the staple drink is more likely to have been beer which we find in accounts, one of which is dated to AD 111 and can be connected with the presence of a brewer (*cervesarius*) named Atrectus in another account.[29]

Two other, unusual items deserve particular notice. In one letter, written to the decurion Lucius, the writer records that a friend has sent him 50 oysters from a place called Cordonovi (or -vae, or -via), perhaps to aid recovery from an illness. Cordonovi (?) is a place which we cannot identify but according to Pliny the Elder, oysters were abundant on the coasts of Britain, Richborough (Rutupiae) being a particularly well-known source; they travelled well and are quite commonly found at military sites in Britain and elsewhere.[30] Perhaps rather more surprising is the appearance of *piper* (pepper) which must have been a really expensive luxury, especially on the northern frontier, and the purchase price of 2 *denarii* suggests as much (though a quantity is not given).[31] All this compares well with what we know of the Roman military diet elsewhere and considerably enlarges our knowledge of the range of foodstuffs and the organisation of the supply system. We cannot contradict the view that the diet of the ordinary soldiers was high in fibre and mainly vegetarian, as studies of the sewage at the fort at Bearsden, near Glasgow, have suggested. We can see, however, that the availability and consumption of meat was far from uncommon, even if the officers may have eaten more of it than the ordinary soldiers. The compilation of a straightforward list of all the items mentioned in the Vindolanda tablets will surely confirm the view that 'wherever on the northern frontiers a Roman soldier was stationed he could be sure of a . . . good balanced diet.'[32]

As for clothing, the very first tablet to be discovered at Vindolanda vividly illustrates the casual despatch of such items at a level probably lower than the officer class: the writer records the despatch of twenty pairs of socks, two pairs of sandals and two pairs of underpants (pl. 1).[33] The provision of goods of this kind is abundantly paralleled in the papyri from Egypt. There is less information, however, about the manufacture of military clothing and related equipment for the unit at large. Although a great deal of footwear was found in the *praetorium* it remains uncertain whether there were facilities for tanning on site. There were certainly facilities for repair and it is possible that military footwear was made in the camp from leather which had been processed elsewhere, perhaps at Catterick. This would fit the evidence of the military report which places 12 shoemakers in the workshops and the account which records a quantity of *clavi caligares* (nails for boots). Another account which records purchases by ordinary soldiers from three named centuries contains *sudaria* (napkins or towels), *sebum* (tallow, probably used as soap) and *corrigiae* (thongs). Military pay-records from Egypt make it clear that standard deductions were made from the soldiers' pay for essential pieces of clothing and equipment but it looks as if the particular items in this account were extras, at least some of which are appropriate to the context of the bath-house.[34]

The movement of small sums of money between individuals is well-attested. Octavius mentions credit arrangements for the small sum of 8½ *denarii* between himself, Tertius and Fatalis. An account of cash sums lists receipts of 34 *denarii* including payments from individuals followed by a list of outstanding debts of 20 *denarii* from further individuals or groups. Yet another may contain a record of the repayment of a loan and a letter explicitly refers to such a debt. A third records, and in some cases cancels, sums received as whole or part payments for particular purchases, including a horse and some iron.[35]

Travel and the exchange of visits were perhaps not confined to the officer class. The letters which soldiers sent to the prefect requesting leave (*commeatus*) sometimes specify the place at which the leave was to be spent – on one occasion Coria (Corbridge), on another Ulucium (location unknown). This must surely be put in the context of the existence of familial and friendship groups which must partly originate in common geographical background. But the movement of units and parts of units, as well as the transfer of individuals between units, will also have played a part in creating or maintaining such contacts. This appears to be the nature of the social network which is evident in the letter of Chrauttius to Veldeius, the governor's groom. Noteworthy features include the gentle reproach, which presupposes a regular correspondence between Chrauttius and Veldeius, as does the reference to news from the *parentes* (probably to be taken as 'elders' rather than literal parents) who may not be in Britain, the greeting *uerbis meis*, the practical matter of the shears, the second-hand communication with Virilis, and greetings transmitted to other friends or relations. What is particularly striking about all this is the extent to which it reflects social life and the centrality of such relationships in the concerns of the writers and correspondents.[36]

It was, of course, the existence of the military establishment which enabled the community to maintain such contacts and to embellish its lifestyle in this way not least, as we shall see in more detail in the next chapter, by providing and encouraging the literate environment in which they were able to communicate. They nevertheless offer us some opportunity to appreciate the domestic comforts and amenities available in a relatively undeveloped frontier region. Comparisons with Kipling's India will, of course, spring to mind, just as they lie behind much of what he wrote about the Romans in northern Britain. It is clear that the evidence from Vindolanda presupposes the existence of civilian settlement, in some form, in close proximity, and there is some evidence for the presence of women and children inside the fort during the barracks period, as well in the *praetorium*.[37] How many of the traders were civilians we simply cannot tell, but the petition or draft letter which complains of the beating administered to the writer reads as if it comes from someone who is not a soldier. It is striking that he describes himself as a *homo trasmarinus* (a man from overseas) and underlines the fact that at this period we cannot certainly show at Vindolanda the presence of native Britons in the penumbra of the military literates.[38] This picture of the officers' lifestyle, albeit incomplete and patchy, is, of course, very far from the senatorial and equestrian milieu of Pliny's letters but it is a remarkably reasonable facsimile. Its adoption by Batavian élites is important because it gave them access to privilege and status in the Roman social hierarchy As for those below this rank, it is difficult to know how attractive the lifestyle of the Roman soldier in the far north might be. One tantalising fragment in the correspondence of Cerialis may have a reference to *desertores* (deserters) and there is another text in which the detention of deserters may be reported.[39] Soldiers were inevitably subject to the rigorous discipline of an establishment in which the military officers were prominent authority figures in the administration of justice. Two fragmentary texts appear to refer to the delivery of petitions (*libelli*) to Cerialis and to the holding of a hearing (*cognitio*), respectively. We may also have a petition about the case of a stolen belt or baldric (*balteus*), perhaps in a servile context.[40]

Nevertheless, the availability at Vindolanda of the creature comforts which we have discussed might persuade us to paint a less bleak picture than that imagined by W. H. Auden:[41]

> Over the heather the wet wind blows,
> I've lice in my tunic and a cold in my nose.
>
> the rain comes pattering out of the sky,
> I'm a Wall soldier, I don't know why.
>
> The mist creeps over the hard grey stone,
> my girl's in Tungria; I sleep alone.
>
> When I'm a veteran with only one eye
> I shall do nothing but look at the sky.

If he had lice, there were baths, soap and towels, for the cold, a medical service and a hospital; if looking at the sky gave him inflammation of the eyes, he could sign on the sick-list. If he was lonely he could take leave and find a friend in Corbridge, or perhaps even go home to Tungria. But it would be optimistic to suppose that even the Roman army could stop the rain pattering out of the sky in a climate notorious for its *tempestates molestae*.[42]

NOTES

1 **13**. The evidence for domestic life discussed in this chapter may be compared with the material collected and discussed by Allason-Jones (1989), chs 4–5.

2 Tableware of Gallus, *BGU* III 781 with Oliver and Shelton (1979). On the terms for different kinds of vessels see Strong (1966), 128–30.

3 *VRR* I.

4 E. Birley (1988), 147–64. Caution is required in applying the analogy, however, since the appointment of a Batavian noble to command a Batavian unit was quite different from the usual pattern of appointment to equestrian commands and might have been for a longer period.

5 *VRR* I.

6 See Rawson (ed. 1986), chs 1, 7 (further bibliographical information on p. 254).

7 **10**. It is possible that the word *allatus* (line 16) is also the name of a slave.

8 Imperial household, Weaver (1972). Soldiers' slaves, M. P. Speidel (1989). Slave sale, *ChLA* III 200. Candidus, **25**. Rhenus, *Tab. Vindol.* II 347. Slave of Verecundus, **26**. The centurion's slaves, **20**.i.7.

9 *Tab. Vindol.* II 322.

10 **10**. For Massic wine see Pliny, *Natural History*, 14.64.

11 **11**. For sheep at Vindolanda see Hodgson (1977), *VRR* III, 110–1. Gallic diet, Trow (1990), 107, King (1991).

12 The references in boldface are, as elsewhere, to the texts as numbered in Appendix II. The others designate publication numbers in *Tab. Vindol.* II.

13 Account of Gavo, **12**. 'Shopping-list' (?), *Tab. Vindol.* II 193. Letter to Candidus, **25**. Letter to slave of Verecundus, **26**. Letter to Brocchus, *Tab. Vindol.* II 233. Recipe (?), *Tab. Vindol.* II 208.

14 Account of clothing, *Tab. Vindol.* II 207. Letter of Super, **20**. Letter of Cerialis, **17**. Loan, *Tab. Vindol.* II 206. Purchases on a journey, *Tab. Vindol.* II 185. *victoriati*, *Tab. Vindol.* II 323. On the use of coin in the Roman empire see Howgego (1992).

15 **14**, *Tab. Vindol.* II 195, 197. Account of Gavo, **12**. Thorigny inscription, *AJ* 140.13. For textiles at Vindolanda see *VRR* III, 76–90, with further bibliography.

16 *VRR* III, 31–7, 76–90. For comment on this and other points concerning the clothing I am grateful to Dr J.-P. Wild.

17 For the small finds see *VRR* IV. Rings, *Tab. Vindol.* II 196.back 5.

18 Diocletian's Edict, Lauffer (1971).

19 Correspondence of Terentianus *CEL* 141–8. Collections of ostraka, *CEL* 73–80 and *O. Claud.*

20 Payments *ad sacrum* etc., **10**. Sacrifice, *Tab. Vindol.*II 265. New Year's greeting, *Tab. Vindol.* II 261. Calendar from Doura-Europos, *RMR* 117.

21 **25**. For the significance of the Saturnalia for slaves see Macrobius, *Saturnalia* 1.10.20.

22 **6**.10. Perhaps Nether Denton, see Jones and Mattingly (1990), 275 and cf. G. D. B. Jones (1990).

23 *Tab. Vindol.* II 313.

24 Invitation, **21**. Draft letter, *Tab. Vindol.* II 227. Medicine, *Tab. Vindol.* II 294.

25 Account of food, **10**. Letter of Severa, **22**. Briga, *PNRB* 277–8; inscription, *RIB* 2022.

26 **16**. Micianus, *RIB* 1041. Relief, Bruce (1875), no.243.

27 Paterna, *Tab. Vindol.* II 294. Valatta, *Tab. Vindol.* II 257. The *familia*, see note 6, above.

28 Account of wheat, **6**. Bread, Davies (1989), 191.

29 Lard, **8**.i.7. Livestock, **6**, *Tab. Vindol.* II 183. Meat, see Davies (1989), 191–3. Beer, *Tab. Vindol.* II 186. Brewer, **8**.ii.14.

30 Oysters, **24**. Pliny, *Natural History* 9.169, cf. Juvenal 4.140. Davies (1989), 193–4.

31 **9**.i.4.

32 Dickson (1989).

33 **34**.

34 Footwear, *VRR* III, 31–46. Shoemakers, **2**.2. Nails, *Tab. Vindol.* II 186.7–8. Napkins etc., **9**. Pay-record, *RMR* 68.

35 Octavius, **32**.ii.21–3. Account of debts, **7**. Loan, *Tab. Vindol.* II 206. Letter mentioning a debt, **30** (cf. Tomlin (1992)). Account, **8**.

36 Leave, **5**, *Tab. Vindol.* II 166–77. Letter of Chrauttius, **28**.

37 For the footwear see *VRR* III, 31–6. The *contubernalis* mentioned in **7**.14 may be an unofficial 'wife'.

38 **33**.

39 *Tab. Vindol.* II 226, 320

40 *Tab. Vindol.* II 281, 317. *Balteus*, *Tab. Vindol.* II 322.

41 'Roman Wall Blues,' W. H. Auden, *Collected poems* (London, 1976), 121.

42 **17**.

7

LETTERS AND LITERACY

At Vindolanda in about AD 100 Flavius Cerialis, prefect of the Ninth Cohort of Batavians, sat and drafted a letter to one Crispinus in which he attempted to gain access to the patronage of the provincial governor. Towards the end of the draft he states specifically *haec tibi a Vindolanda scribo* ('I am writing this to you from Vindolanda'): no phrase in all our texts stimulates the imagination more vividly or reminds us more emphatically that the environment at Vindolanda was a literate one.[1] From the point of view of acculturation and romanisation, perhaps the most important and exciting aspect of the tablets is that they illuminate the extent, the quality and the nature of literacy in the community at Vindolanda and, to a lesser extent, at those places from which letters came to members of the community at Vindolanda. We may also consider the extent to which the information they offer is more broadly applicable in the Roman world of the period around AD 100. It is not merely a question of quantification of the number of people in a society who were able to achieve whatever we consider an adequate ability to read and write. On this subject the tablets probably reflect, like other material, a small proportion of the population which was fully literate; it is important to remember, however, that there are degrees of literacy. Attempts at quantifying and measuring literacy in the ancient world face formidable difficulties, and it is much more important and fruitful to consider the ways in which use of the written word was embedded in the institutional and social structures of a society and the functions which depended upon that use; in other words, to assess the degree to which the lives and activities of people who could write little or not at all, as well as those of people who could, were controlled by the written word. The relatively small size of the literate group needs to be set against the fact that a much larger proportion of the population behaved according to conventions which depended on the presumption that written communication was a normal means of regulating society. To that extent, we could assert, even without the evidence of Vindolanda, that the

Roman civilisation was a literate one. What we can study at Vindolanda, through a collection of evidence of unique coherence and depth, is the character of that literacy at the periphery of the Roman world and its role in the organisation of that provincial region and society.[2]

Enough has already been said to assure us that at Vindolanda the writing of official and private documents and letters was absolutely standard and existed over virtually the whole period of the pre-Hadrianic occupation. But it is hard for us to recall now that the mere existence of these thin leaves of wood bearing writing in ink came as a considerable surprise when they were first found in 1973, especially in such quantities. The archaeological record of the Roman world, in fact, reveals two or three examples previously known (including one from London) which might have been interpreted as an aberration from what was thought to be the standard practice of using stilus tablets in areas where papyrus was not readily available. In 1973, however, it became apparent that a mass of documentation on leaf tablets must originally have existed at many sites in the north-western provinces – this is guaranteed not merely by probability but by the fact that much of the correspondence found at Vindolanda was written at other places and by the discovery of examples from other sites in recent years.[3] The existence of this mass of documentation and correspondence in a geographical context in which the indigenous culture was at best only proto-literate is a fact of major importance. It might have been thought, after all, that the level of documentation which we find in military circles in Egypt and Syria owed something to the already literate context (even if the military documentation there is largely in Latin and the established literacy is in Greek), but this is now hardly plausible.[4] If a literate military establishment appears on the northern frontier of Britain within a decade or two of its occupation by the Romans, then it must have been universal in the Roman provinces.

An influential factor whose importance is harder to assess is the technological. Papyrus, it might be argued, was plentiful and generally available in Egypt and throughout the east, where use of the written word was thus materially supported and facilitated. So too in the military milieu where the technology existed to manufacture these tablets. How far this is true outside the military sphere of influence is a different matter.

These leaf tablets are mentioned and described by classical authors – the most explicit help comes from a passage in the historian Herodian who describes them as thin leaves of lime-wood made to be folded with the writing on the inner faces. The lime was not native to northern Britain in this period; our tablets are made of birch and alder (and occasionally oak), which do grow locally. Manufacture was presumably simple, given the technology available to make fine veneers for furniture, for example; the tablets are cut from the wood, not the bark of the tree. By contrast, the stilus tablets were probably imported ready-made. The availability of leaf tablets thus means that writing was not restricted to those who could afford expensive materials. Not that they are simply casual offcuts – they are clearly purpose made, as is shown by the fact that they often have pierced tie-holes and v-shaped, or occasionally semi-circular, notches in the edges, made before the leaf was used (as is shown by the fact that writers space their texts so as to avoid them). There is some variation in the size of the leaf tablets: the thickness ranges between 0.25mm and 3mm; the largest tablets are generally about the size of a postcard (though the strength report of the Tungrians is a good deal larger than this), the smallest about half the size. It is clear, nevertheless, that we have a simple manufacturing technology which is disciplined and functional, enabling texts to be written outside the context of an official record-office. The number of letters which came to Vindolanda from other places makes it clear that this phenomenon is widespread.[5]

Widespread familiarity with the medium is one aspect of the diffusion of literacy, familiarity with the format and method of conveying the message another. Habits of use and methods of writing do not develop randomly, but within the framework of conventions and expectations. The documents and the letters from Vindolanda are very illuminating in this respect because they tell us a great deal about the conventions and the ways in which writers can employ variation in using them.

Documents and accounts tend naturally to be formalised, although less so in the Vindolanda tablets than in the papyri from Doura-Europos, for instance, many of which clearly come from the official record-office of the military unit. The strength report of the Tungrian cohort is written on a very large leaf, with the writing running across the grain and parallel to the short edge. Other, much shorter duty reports are written along the grain, as are the brief reports which are headed by the word *renuntium*. More often than not accounts are written in narrow columns, *transversa charta*, that is, with the leaf turned through 90 degrees and the writing parallel to the short edge. The most interesting evidence of the use of wooden leaves as writing material is supplied by a long account on several leaves which were joined together in a concertina format, offering us a completely unique example of a wooden notebook. It is this kind of notebook which is probably denoted by the Latin word *pugillaria* used frequently in the writings of the contemporary poets Martial and Juvenal. This unique concertina format certainly cannot be described as a primitive form of codex but it could have been a medium not only for notebooks but also for early literary works, to which the phrase, commonly found in ancient manuscripts, *liber explicit* ('the book ends here') would be peculiarly appropriate. The method of writing accounts in narrow columns, *transversa charta*, is obviously explicable and logical, but not universal – among finds from the latest period is an account of commodities including soap and towels which is written in three columns along the grain, with the central column straddling the fold; so here the fold has no psychological effect. We also have examples of accounts written on both sides of the leaf and in the two-column format more characteristic of the letters.[6] Some of the accounts relate to the domestic administration of the *praetorium*, rather than the unit as a whole, and raise the question of how far the standardisation and format of official military documents influenced the writing of private texts and vice versa, a matter which will also be considered in relation to the palaeography of our texts.

From the point of view of format the letters are perhaps more interesting. In most cases, the writer of a letter takes a leaf of wood which is generally more or less the size of a modern postcard and, with the broad dimension running horizontally, writes the text in two columns, the first column at the left, the second at the right. The columns are often not of equal width, the left-hand being frequently broader than the right and extending beyond the centre of the leaf. The opening address generally occupies the first two lines of the left-hand column and the closing valediction normally comes at the bottom of the right-hand column but this will depend, of course, on the length of the message. The closure is often but not always written by a second hand, which must be the hand of the author (as opposed to the 'scribe') of the letter. In some cases a closure is written by the first hand and the second hand adds a simple *uale* or *uale frater* after it.[7] After the letter has been written the leaf is scored vertically down the centre and folded. The address is then written on the back of the right-hand half; the name of the addressee is in large, spindly letters, the name of the sender, written below with *a* or *ab* ('from'), is in normal cursive, but almost always sloping upwards from left to right.[8]

This pattern is not confined to a single group of letters, a single period, one group of writers or correspondents or one provenance. It is by far the commonest letter-format, but it was not universal and the variations in the Vindolanda material are very interesting. First, the leaf may be used in different ways. A letter may be written on two or three leaves, folded together. The first part of a letter from Claudia Severa is written in one column across the whole leaf, the remainder on second and third leaves in two columns and the closing greeting is actually on the back. Octavius writes to Candidus on two leaves, two columns on each leaf, but the sequence runs from right to left and is best explained by the supposition that Octavius was a left-hander.[9] Some writers conclude their text by writing at a right-angle down the left-hand margin or between the columns, others continue on the back of the leaf, perhaps not only in drafts of which Cerialis' letter to Crispinus is the clearest example. The address is once written on the back of the left-hand half of the leaf.[10]

Second, the layout and appearance of the text: in by far the majority of cases the first line of the text contains the name of the author and the addressee, sometimes with *suo*; the second line contains *salutem* or *suo salutem* at the far right. In one case the whole address is written on the first line and there are also a few variations in position. In one case the address on the back is written not in the usual elongated letters but in ordinary cursive.[11] There is, as far as I know, no ancient text which describes the proper layout of a letter, though there are instructions for composing particular kinds of letters such as *litterae commendaticiae* (of which there is one substantial example at Vindolanda). The relationship between these features of layout in our Vindolanda letters and the layout of a 'literary' letter is a question of major interest – our sometimes elaborate opening addresses do not appear in the latter. Since literary figures like Cicero and Pliny normally wrote on papyrus, a comparison between the letters from Vindolanda and surviving examples on Greek and Latin papyri should be significant. The presence of tie-holes and notches in the wooden tablets is not relevant and papyrus letters were normally rolled or folded in thin strips and were sometimes sealed. The manner in which addresses are written on the back of the papyrus is closely comparable, however, to what we find in the Vindolanda letters. The double column layout, with the left broader than the right, can be paralleled in papyrus letters (both Greek and Latin) but it is comparatively very rare.[12] There are, it must be admitted, not enough Latin papyri to make a significant comparison possible, but it is interesting to consider whether the technical and formal aspects of Latin texts on wooden leaves are characteristic of that particular medium.

Equally interesting are the practices of abbreviation and punctuation, notably the use of oblique strokes, known as apices, over vowels, and interpunction between words, as well as word division by simple spacing. For *noster*, *n* with a superscript bar is common, as are the standard abbreviations *n* for *numerus* and *m* for *modius*, normally with a superscript bar but the latter once with an oblique. The title *praefectus* is invariably written as *praef*, almost always without any mark of abbreviation. In her birthday invitation, Claudia Severa (or her scribe) abbreviates her *gentilicium* Claudia to *Cl*, the only such clear example in the addresses. This letter certainly also shows a wider use of apices than has been regarded as the norm and not merely for long vowels. It is difficult to understand why it is used over short vowels and even more extraordinary that there is a similiar mark which appears occasionally and seems to be used as punctuation. The employment of interpunction is frequent in a few texts, occasional in a few more and absent from most, which seems to confirm the belief that its use was generally in decline at this time. In one interesting example the second hand which wrote the closing greeting assiduously imitated the first writer's use of interpunction.[13] The use of spacing between words, which is the commonest form of punctuation in Latin texts, is equally capricious – some writers do it consistently but the fact that the majority do not suggests that it was not thought essential for the appearance of a text or as a condition of ability to read and understand it. The writers of the texts found at Vindolanda seem to have operated with a broad commonality of conventions without being rigidly confined to standard practices; but they also employ conventions which have not hitherto been commonly found elsewhere.

Overall, the evidence of the Vindolanda tablets suggests that technology is less of a limiting factor than we might have thought in the spread of literacy. On the other hand, the diffusion of literate skills seems to take place within a framework of broadly standard conventions some of which can, so far as a comparison with the evidence of the papyri will take us, be detected at the other end of the empire. It looks as if the recipient of a letter or the user of an account would in general terms know what to expect to see, but this does not mean that there is no room for individuality and manipulation of the medium and the appearance of the message; the layout of Octavius' letter with the first and third columns on the right and the second and fourth on the left is, however, perhaps more paradoxical than one might expect to find in a modern literacy.[14] The standardisation of particular forms emerges from a literate milieu which is characterised by a breadth of practice but it may still be one in which the *sort* of thing which people read and write is constrained. The letter of Octavius and many other examples have to be set against the implications of rigidity and restrictiveness implied by the idea of an institutionalised 'chancery'.

The existence of patterns is of course relevant to the question of how many different people were actually writing texts. It would be less surprising to find standard patterns if there were only a few clerks or scribes who were writing these documents and letters. But what is truly astonishing about the Vindolanda collection is the immense number of individual hands represented. In the tablets discovered in the 1970s more than eighty different hands were identified and in the material from the 1980s there are several hundred more. Of course, this is to be expected in the letters, most of which originate elsewhere, but even among those texts which we know to have been written at Vindolanda there are very few indeed which may be the work of one hand. A small group of accounts from the *praetorium* might be work of a single person. The twenty-seven formulaic reports with the *renuntium* heading are almost all attributed to Period 3 and are all written in different hands. With chits following a more or less identical formula it would have been simple to devise a form which the reporting officer merely had to sign or authenticate in some way, but it seems much more likely that the individual *optiones* wrote the reports themselves. Similarly, the dozen texts requesting leave (*commeatus*) in a more or less standard formula are, in striking contrast to a similar text from Egypt, not simply forms with a blank for the name to be inserted, but letters written in different hands, some of them quite good and coming, we may assume, from soldiers in the lower ranks.[15]

As for the correspondence, we probably have eighteen drafts, copies or letters which come from Flavius Cerialis himself and there are probably seven different hands represented. The one hand which is common to eight letters or groups of fragments is probably that of Cerialis himself. There are two other hands which may each appear in more than one draft or copy.[16] The two letters from Claudia Severa to Lepidina, Cerialis' wife, are written by different scribes.[17] It is worth adding that although most of our letters were not written by their authors but by clerks or amanuenses, the authors normally add the closing greetings (which show some variety of expression) in their own hands. The most striking example is the end of Severa's birthday invitation which concludes with three lines in her own hand (and is paralleled in two other texts); this is much longer and more elaborate than any other example of the closure of a letter.[18] The point does not need to be laboured; the authors of these letters, including the women, were in the technical sense basically literate, even if they had amanuenses to write the bulk of their letters; we shall shortly see that their literacy actually went beyond the technicalities. The general point which clearly emerges from the diversity in use of materials and expression is one which can be made simply and emphatically: the authors and writers were masters of their material, not the other way round, and this is one very significant indication of the *quality* of their literacy.

This impression is strongly reinforced by a detailed study of the palaeography of these texts. It is fair to say that in no field do the Vindolanda texts make a more important (and potentially revolutionary) contribution to knowledge. It is hard to overemphasise the value of a dated body of material of such variety which comes from a part of the Roman world hitherto unrepresented in our evidence and at the opposite pole from the area which has given us most, namely Egypt.[19]

The first thing to emphasise is that these hundreds of examples of different hands give us an immense variety of individual scripts of different character, ranging from fluent and elegant to stiff and clumsy, with everything in between. At the same time, it is apparent from a detailed comparison of these scripts with the evidence from Egypt that the handwriting as a whole is basically of the same type as that in the Latin papyri. It is of fundamental importance that Vindolanda has enabled us to say with confidence, first that it is overwhelmingly likely that at the time pen-and-ink cursive Latin was being written in the same way all over the empire, and second, that within this broad classification there was a huge range of individuality (much as one might expect to find in a modern literate society). Of course, we must again be wary of exaggerating the social spectrum which is represented, for much of the Latin material from Egypt, like all of that from Vindolanda, emanates from military circles.

It is instructive to move from these generalities to consideration of some particular points. As we have seen, some of the palaeographical conventions, such as the use of abbreviation and interpunction, reveal close kinship with texts from the other end of the empire. For a proper appreciation of the kind of writing which we are dealing with, the analysis of individual letter-forms is of particular importance. These have to be considered in the general context of the history of Latin handwriting which concerns two main types of writing – capital and cursive. At Vindolanda, we have a few important examples of capital scripts or bookhands which are directly related to the kind of writing found in manuscripts of literary works and are traceable right through the imperial period and into the early Middle Ages. The majority of our texts, however, are written in cursive of the kind usually called Old Roman Cursive which was predominant in the Roman world until the third century AD. This type includes not only the normal writing in our letters and documents but also the script used for addresses, which is better regarded as a variant of cursive rather than a capital script. In the course of the third century AD, ORC was replaced by a type of cursive known as New Roman Cursive (NRC) with several characteristic letter forms which are crucially different from those of ORC. Indeed, the relationship between ORC and NRC has been a matter of great discussion by palaeographers for it is generally agreed that there are some letter forms in NRC which simply cannot have come into being as variations or developments of the normal ORC forms. The question is, where did they come from? Some have related them directly to the capital 'bookhands' rather than the ORC forms. Others have suggested a more complex development: for example, that from the earliest times there is a difference between official cursive, which we might expect to find in documents, and private script, written by the educated classes; that it was the private script which was joined by a more elementary 'popular script', written to a great extent by self-taught people using simple capital forms as their models and the coalescence of the two produced NRC.

This is only one of several possible explanations of the relationship and our Vindolanda texts cannot provide a solution to the problem when it is put in this form – for one thing they are too early in date. But they do invite us to consider the range of letter forms appearing *c.* AD 100 and the relationships between them. There are several examples of letter forms which, if earlier theories based on sparse evidence were correct, really ought not to appear at this date at all and some of them *do* seem to be related to NRC forms. More striking, indeed absolutely astonishing, is the appearance in a capital text, of a form of *e* which had hitherto appeared only in incised texts (stylus tablets or graffiti) and may be related to the NRC form.[20] In general, we are struck by the mixture of forms which others have tended to classify more exclusively as private, popular or official, even in one and the same text, so these distinctions appear to us less than clear-cut. Of course, we are bound to reflect on the probability that many private letters were being written or copied by people accustomed to writing official documents and that many 'private' writers may have learned to write from those people or at least have been in close contact with them. Some of the letters, indeed, are difficult to classify by subject-matter as exclusively official or private. It has been natural to suppose that the military bureaucracy was an important influence in the spread of literacy. No doubt this is valid, but the evidence for the presence of literacy in the domestic setting of the *praetorium* should alert us to the possibility that the influences may flow in two directions.

There is another general consideration which points in the same direction, which highlights the relationship, or at least the contact, between capital and cursive hands. Normally these are studied in different kinds of texts, literary and documentary respectively. Scholars have occasionally commented that the development of capital hands might be illuminated by consideration of the headings in military texts, principally pay-records. Vindolanda provides several examples in which writers switch from capital to cursive in the body of one text: once for a consular date, on other occasions for headings or notes of different kinds, but writing each with equal facility; it is particularly noticeable that this tends to occur in accounts or financial texts. Further, among the cursive hands, it is possible to describe some as literary or almost literary in character and there is one thoroughly cursive but strikingly calligraphic text which is, in fact, a routine military report. Finally, it is of immense importance that the Vindolanda tablets present us with the earliest known examples of shorthand writing in Latin, probably in a system which is known from later antiquity and called 'Tironian notes' (after Cicero's freedman secretary, Tiro). It has been argued that the development and use of shorthand are likely to derive from the military environment. Here we have it cheek by jowl with other kinds of writing, in the context not of the official record-office, but the commanding officer's residence. This is a point of absolutely crucial importance for it suggests the intermix of what are thought to be parallel developments in a milieu which was primarily military but included, as we have seen, the officers' extended *familia*, literate women, slaves and possibly traders or artisans as well.[21]

This may help us to illuminate the relationship between the different kinds of writing in the process of learning to become literate. All seem to have been commonly in use in the army, which was certainly one school for provincials along with schools like those which had been established for the children of Gallic nobles at Autun and, more recently, by Agricola in Britain. The progression will run from the record of the military essentials to an aspiration to 'polite letters'. On the margins, so to speak, we might note the existence of two rather primitive drawings. In the *praetorium* at Vindolanda, probably during the occupation by Cerialis and his family, someone took a writing-tablet on which a private letter had been begun, but not finished, and wrote on the back of it in a rather good, but degenerating, capital hand a line from the *Aeneid* of Virgil (9.473): a complete line, not a complete sentence and certainly not a readily memorable one, from the second half of the poem which is generally much less in evidence as a quarry for writing exercises; and one with the remarkable form of *e*, hitherto unparalleled in ink texts (pl. III). Are texts of Virgil available at Vindolanda? Are they used for writing practice (as is commonly found on papyri) and by whom? Cerialis' children? There is a limit to the value of speculation and we may yet learn more. But the existence of this text is perhaps the single most remarkable phenomenon of our find. It may, indeed, not be the only literary text at Vindolanda (even if it is the only one of which we can be certain) and one of the fragmentary letters carries a clear reference to 'books' (*libros*). If the imagination may be tickled by a remarkable coincidence, it is worth adding that almost on the same day as the Vindolanda text came to light, a batch of Latin military papyri from Herod's fortress at Masada in Israel was found to include a scrap containing a line from the fourth book of the *Aeneid*.[22]

The ability and the need to write official documents are no doubt the foundation for the composition of more personal texts, just as it is the need for military communication which provides the facility for sending letters to people, letters in which the official and the personal concerns are not always segregated. Having established the notion of a basic technical literacy which extended from the unit's record-office to at least the individual officers and the members of their households, we can appreciate the fundamental way in which the military establishment enabled the community to embellish its lifestyle by providing and encouraging the literate environment in which they were able to communicate. We might go further and say that the lifestyle is part of a political and cultural dominance which could not have been sustained without the literate environment. Our appreciation of the symbiosis is enhanced by the existence, particularly in the correspondence of Cerialis, of drafts and complete versions of his own letters, showing the extent to which the bureaucratic habit extended into the private sphere. Drafts can be recognised by the absence of opening and closing formulae or erasures; complete versions of letters from him may indicate that a perfect copy of the final version was made too, for it is surely less likely that these were top copies which found their way back to Vindolanda or were never sent.

Next, we may consider the extent and quality of their literacy in the broader sense: what thoughts did they put into written words and how did they express themselves? One obvious indicator of the degree of individuality in the letters is the extent of the opening and closing formulae of the letters. As I have already remarked, the closing greetings are normally written by the author of the letter in his or her own hand; the address is by the same hand which writes the body of the text, but we will want to ask whether the content and composition of the body of the text should be credited to the author. The addresses show little variation from the basic and standard *Claudius Karus Ceriali suo salutem*

('Claudius Karus to his Cerialis, greetings'). For instance: *Chrauttius Veldeio suo fratri contubernali antiquo plurimam salutem* ('Chrauttius to Veldeius, his brother and old messmate, very many greetings'), *Sollemnis Paridi fratri plurimam salutem* ('Sollemnis to his Paris, very many greetings'), *Vittius Adiutor aquilifer leg(ionis) ii Aug(ustae) Cassio Saeculari fraterclo suo plurimam [salutem]* ('Vittius Adiutor eagle-bearer of the Second Augustan legion to Cassius Saecularis, his little brother, very many greetings'), an example remarkable for its fullness and formality.[23] There is more individuality in the closing greetings, even though they are mostly variations on a standard theme: *vale frater* ('farewell brother') and *vale domine frater* ('farewell my lord and brother') are the simplest. We also find, for example: *opto sis felicissimus quod es dignissimus* ('I pray that you may enjoy the best of fortune because you are most worthy'); the uncommon *opto felicissimus vivas* ('I pray that you may live in the best of fortune'), *opto bene valere te domine vale* ('I pray that you are in good health, my lord; farewell'). Most striking of all is the elaborate and elegant expression of Claudia Severa to Lepidina: *vale soror anima mea ita ualeam karissima et have* ('farewell, sister, my dearest soul, as I hope to prosper, and hail'), employing a somewhat convoluted usage of *ita ualeam* which may be taken with *karissima* or with *ita* looking back to *uale*, and the very rare *have* added at the end. Severa appears to be fond of fulsome closures of this kind, for another of her letters ends similarly, addressing the recipient (probably Lepidina again) as *anima ma* (sc. *mea*) *desideratissima* ('my most longed-for soul').[24]

As for the substantive content of the letters, the invitation from Claudia Severa is certainly the work of a professional writer, but the elegance of the Latin may well be due to Severa herself, as the closure suggests; her other letter, written by another amanuensis, is also very good. The letter of recommendation from Karus to Cerialis shows striking similarities of expression to other documentary examples of *litterae commendaticiae* but it does not woodenly reproduce formulae; on the other hand the Latinity of the letter is rather substandard. By contrast, the draft letter from Cerialis, written in a hand which is surely his own, is exceptional for the quality of the Latin which has a literary flavour and some elegance – manifestly the work of an elegant stylist. Cerialis is working at it, for the erasures show that it does not flow entirely naturally. We have no way of knowing to what extent this is attributable to Batavian thought-patterns, the need to translate or difficulty in manipulating the Latin language.[25] The quality of the corrected draft, however, strongly suggests that Cerialis is by no means out of his depth.

Refinement of thought and expression accompanies civilised social habits, as is evident, for instance, in the New Year's greeting to Cerialis. More commonplace thoughts which accompany practical messages may be well expressed, as in the letter from Chrauttius which certainly takes us to a level below that of the equestrian officer class. Or the even more elaborately phrased reproach in the letter from Sollemnis to Paris: *ut scias me recte valere quod te invicem fecisse cupio, homo inpientissime, qui mihi ne unam epistulam misisti sed puto me humanius facere qui tibi scribo* ('I want you to know that I am in very good health, as I hope you are in turn, you neglectful man, who have sent me not even one letter. But I think that I am behaving in a more considerate fashion in writing to you'); it certainly does not reach Cerialis' standard and shows awkwardness in the use of *ne . . . unam* and *inpientissime*.[26]

Some other aspects of the quality of the Latin deserve attention, for the language of our texts might tell us something about the state of Latin as it was currently spoken and written by these people. The establishment of schools by Agricola might have begun to bear fruit, but since none of our texts can be shown to be the work of native Britons, our evidence will bear on the Latin used by the natives of northern Gaul. As well as the occasional archaism (*salvom, quom, occassionem*), there is enough of a scattering of vulgarised forms and usages which generally confirm developments placed in this period. Retention of the gemination of *s* (for example, in *missi* for *misi*), which is thought largely to have disappeared by this time, is a common feature of the Vindolanda texts; so is a contracted verb form like *rescripsti* for *rescripsisti*. There are traces of vulgar pronunciation changes, ie, for example, *it quot* for *id quod*. And unexpected usages occur: the sense of *sperabo* in Severa's letter and the use of *tot tempus* in that of Chrauttius.[27] In general, we seem to be dealing with a good knowledge of written and spoken Latin which shows signs of the standard or common vulgar usages of the period. Whether the difference in the quality of Latin between the letter of recommendation from Karus and those of Cerialis (assuming that both were responsible for the composition of their missives) reveals a difference in the social stratum from which they came is another matter. It may be observed, however, that if the letter of Octavius to Candidus reflects the milieu of the centurion or the *optio*, the quality of the Latin is good, albeit without achieving the elegance of which Flavius Cerialis was capable.

With all allowance for variation duly made, in general it is clear that many of the letters written by these people, some certainly not officers, were capable of considerable refinement of thought and expression in good Latin. How many of the authors, as distinct from the scribes, were responsible for the wording and composition of their texts is difficult to assess. It looks as if Cerialis certainly composed his own letters (even though the address to Crispinus in his draft is left in a form which would have to be expanded in the fair copy) and it seems probable that Lepidina did so too. This is supported by the fact that one of Cerialis' letters gives us a clear example of a dictation error, in which the scribe wrote *tempestates et hiem* and then erased *et hiem* and replaced it with *etiam*.[28] This evidence gives us reason to suppose that in a significant number of examples it was the author, not the scribe, who composed the letter. Conversely, it is very important for our assessment of the spread of literate skills to emphasise that the fact that an author did not physically write the letter himself (or herself) does not by any means indicate that he (or she) was incapable of doing so.

This is one way in which the writers attempt to personalise their letters, as St Paul did. It is worth dwelling for a while on the sense of immediacy which the writers sometimes attempt to convey in other ways too. Sollemnis addresses Paris as *homo inpientissime*; another writer begins a letter with the unceremonious and acerbic *opto tibi male eveniat* ('I hope it may turn out badly for you'), attempting to convey authority. A third contains the extraordinary expression *per silvolas repto* ('I am lingering in the thickets') in a context where it is unclear whether this is supposed to be taken literally or metaphorically.[29] These can be contrasted with the more elegant and formal Latin found in Cerialis' draft and the more matter-of-fact forms of expression which occur when writers deal with business matters in rather neutral language. From the point of view of cognition it is more interesting to look at some other expressions. We may note particularly, *saluta . . . verbis meis* ('greet so-and-so in my words'), which seems to be a telling psychological indication of some degree of residual orality, Severa perhaps telling Lepidina that there are some things which she must discuss face-to-face. There are also complaints about correspondents not having written frequently enough (for example, Sollemnis to Paris, Chrauttius to Veldeius).[30] This seems to imply an expectation of a fairly intensive degree of literate communication: the whole body of our correspondence implicates a broad range of people (not just the equestrian officer class) in the literacy-using network.

All this, then, shows the widespread writing of good Latin, with common formats, methods and patterns among the officer class in northern Britain, extending to their wives and their slaves, to their correspondents (wherever they were), into the non-officer class, perhaps even the ranks and then the traders with military connections. We can be fairly certain, too, that literacy extends down to centurions, decurions and *optiones*, people not likely to have been recruited entirely from the propertied classes, but achieving, after their military careers, some degree of upward mobility. Some of these people were certainly from areas only recently 'romanised'.

How far can we generalise from this? We cannot readily make sweeping statements about the depth to which literacy had penetrated the social order by AD 100, but we can emphasise the close comparison with the picture presented by contemporary evidence from the east. We should not readily assume a consistent continuum, though there is surely less literacy in the lower social orders than the higher. The impression is that the picture is more untidy and haphazard the lower one goes down the social scale, and this might be expected in a society where literacy was not spread only through the medium of formal schooling. This is consonant not merely with the picture at Vindolanda but also with important evidence from Egypt which shows that literate soldiers tend to be more numerous in legionary than auxiliary units. What is crucial is the fact that if a considerable quality of literacy existed at the lower levels at Vindolanda, then we might suppose that this literacy, sporadic though it was, determined and controlled the lives and activities of the non-literate to a considerable extent. This is precisely the picture which emerges in Egypt.

We can see in some detail the ways in which the military establishment aided the diffusion of literacy and the reasons for which it did so. The documentation of official military activity in the early empire was integral to the structure and operation of the Roman army. The need to record and tabulate unit strengths, movement of troops, acquisition and dispensation of supplies, is part of the logic of an organisation which depended, for its efficiency and effectiveness, on economy of numbers. By any standards, the Roman army is one of the most economical institutions of antiquity. The effective reduction and domination of large tracts of frontier territory by what amounted, in the end, to no more than a few thousand men depended upon efficiency of communication which enabled the strategic occupation of key points in a complex network of roads and forts, placed to maximise control of large areas of countryside populated by scattered native settlements and to facilitate the introduction of appropriate social and economic habits. These processes had already occurred in northern Gaul in the Augustan and Julio-Claudian periods. The acculturation of the Gauls enabled Rome to use them, at the end of the first century AD, as the instruments of domination in north Britain. The élites of the Gallic provinces eagerly embraced the Roman lifestyle, as described in Chapter 6, which supported and reinforced their position in Roman provincial society.

Our texts do not reveal whether the Gallic troopers felt any affinity with their oppressed British brethren, despite the claims which Tacitus put into the mouth of Calgacus in his speech before the battle of Mons Graupius.[31] In any case, our officers are least likely to have felt any such affinity, as the use of the contemptuous diminutive term *Brittunculi* in one of our texts might suggest. The officers had already developed a lifestyle to which certain Roman institutions and practices were crucial. They were absorbed into the social structure in which successful military careers and the manipulation of channels of patronage were of paramount importance. The Batavian prefect Flavius Cerialis had achieved equestrian rank, which meant the possession of a property qualification of 400,000 sesterces and the marks of social prestige which went with it. If he returned to his native land after his service in Britain, he would be a large fish in that pond. In the meantime, the trappings of his existence in Britain included good food, appropriate clothing and equipment, the presence of his family and household slaves, and modest involvement in a social network where the observance of Roman customs including religious festivals bulked large. The ability to keep his household in order by means of written accounts and records is one part of the picture. The acquaintance with Latin literature and the ability to write Latin prose at his level, or a lower one, supported his high position in the social network.

It is not necessarily to be supposed that Gauls and Batavians who acquired Roman habits of literacy did so entirely entirely from scratch. There is, in fact, a certain amount of evidence to suggest access to some very basic degree of literacy in pre-Roman Gallic society – the presence of Celtic inscriptions, coin legends, and so on.[32] What we do not have is any evidence either for widespread use in the organisation of political and social institutions or for the epiphenomenal literacy – personal communication and dependence on the written word which permeated the social and economic structures of Roman society, or those sections of it which our Vindolanda writers represent. It is in this respect, particularly, that we can contrast the north-western empire with Egypt where the literate habits of the Greek-speaking world had long been developed. In contrasting Roman and Gallic society, then, we are not necessarily polarising the literate and the non-literate, but describing and assessing the uses of literacy and their function over a fairly broad social range. The Vindolanda evidence shows us how swiftly Gauls and Batavians acquired these literate habits and how proficient they became within a very short time. If our evidence took us into the third and fourth centuries we would doubtless be able see how these habits penetrated native British society.[33]

NOTES

1 **15**.24–5.

2 Much of the material in this chapter is discussed in Bowman (1991) and (1994).

3 E.g. at Caerleon, Tomlin (1986); Carlisle, Tomlin (1992).

4 For military documentation see *RMR*. For a broader anthology see Daris (1964). For an interesting linguistic study see Adams (1977).

5 For a summary see Ch.2 and for more detail on the manufacture see *Tab. Vindol.* I, pp. 26–31. For semi-circular notches see *Tab. Vindol.* II 214, 216.

6 Strength report, **1**. Military reports, **4**, *Tab. Vindol.* II 127–53. Accounts written *transversa charta*, **6**, **7**, **10**. Concertina format, **10**, cf. Bowman (1975), Tjäder (1986). Three-column account, **9**. Two-column account, **8**.

7 *vale frater* written by the second hand, **19**.ii.17.

8 On the pattern of addresses see *Tab. Vindol.* II, pp. 43–5.

9 **22**, **32**.

10 Right-angle, **26**, **29**, *Tab. Vindol.* II 316. Back of the leaf, *Tab. Vindol.* II 305, 307; Cerialis to Crispinus, **15**. Address on the left-hand half, *Tab. Vindol.* II 319.

11 Address on first line, *Tab. Vindol.* II 212. Variations in position, **19**, **29**, *Tab. Vindol.* II 259, 275. Address in ordinary cursive, *Tab. Vindol.* II 352.

12 The question of layout is considered by Bischoff (1990), 27–30, but only with reference to books. The literary evidence is cited by Cugusi (1983), 30. Addresses, *P. Dura*, pl. XXXIII. Columns in Greek and Latin papyri, *P. Oxy.* XVIII 2192, *P. Wisc.* II 84, *ChLA* VI 300, X 452, 457, XI 487.

13 Common abbreviations: *noster*, **18**.ii.10, *Tab. Vindol.* II 260.7; *numerus*, **27**; *modius*, **6**, **10**; *praefectus*, **20**; *gentilicium*, **21**.i.1. Use of the apex, **18**, **21**, *Tab. Vindol.* II 265, cf. *Tab. Vindol.* II, pp. 57–61, Wingo (1972), 95–6, Kramer (1991). Interpunction, *Tab. Vindol.* II 297, 345, cf. *Tab. Vindol.* I, p. 69.

14 **32**; the most likely explanation is that Octavius was left-handed.

15 Accounts, **11**, **13**, **14**, *Tab. Vindol.* II 197. Reports, **4**, *Tab. Vindol.* II 127–53. Leave, **5**, *Tab. Vindol.* II 166–77, cf. *O. Flor.* 1.

16 Letters from Cerialis, *Tab. Vindol.* II 225–42; 225–32 are in Cerialis' hand; 234 and 239 appear to be the work of a single hand, 233, 235 and 240 the work of another.

17 **21**, **22**. Both hands seem to be represented in other letters coming from the household of Brocchus and Severa.

18 **21**.ii.11–4.

19 For details see *Tab. Vindol.* I, pp. 51–71, II, pp. 47–54, Thomas (1976) and (1990).

20 In general see Tjäder (1986). Hélène

Cuvigny has kindly informed me that a comparable example occurs in an ink text on an unpublished ostrakon from Mons Claudianus in Egypt.

21 Capital and cursive, *Tab. Vindol.* II 186, 206. Calligraphic report, *Tab. Vindol.* II 152. Shorthand, *Tab. Vindol.*II 122–6.

22 Drawings, *Tab. Vindol.* II 121, R. E. Birley (1990), 32. *Aeneid, Tab. Vindol.* II 118. Other possible literary texts, *Tab. Vindol.* II 119 and 120. Books, *Tab. Vindol.* II 333. Masada, *Doc. Masada* 721; note also the Virgilian writing-exercise in *O. Claud.* 190.

23 *Tab. Vindol.* II 251, **28**, **29**, *Tab. Vindol.* II 214.

24 **19**, *Tab. Vindol.* II 252, 264, **34**, *Tab. Vindol.* II 258, **21**, **22**.

25 Karus to Cerialis, **19**. Draft of Cerialis, **15**.

26 Chrauttius, **28**. Sollemnis, **29**.

27 For detailed discussion of the linguistic phenomena see *Tab. Vindol.* I, pp. 72–4, Adams (1994). *sperabo*, **21**.ii.11. *tot tempus*, **29**.i.5.

28 **17**.

29 Paul, *I Cor.* 16.21. Sollemnis, **29**.i.5–6. *opto* etc., *Tab. Vindol.* II 321.

30 *verbis meis*, **28**.i.10, *Tab. Vindol.* II 353. Severa, **22**.b.ii.3–4. Complaints, **28**, **29**.

31 Above, p. 32.

32 See Woolf (1994).

33 Some indications are given by the Bath curse tablets, from a later period (Tomlin, 1992). There are signs that Vindolanda may eventually yield material from a later period (see *VRR* II, 15).

TECHNICAL TERMINOLOGY

Names

The nomenclature of the Roman citizen consisted of three elements, often referred to as the tria nomina: first, a *praenomen* (forename), such as Marcus, Lucius, Titus; second, a *gentilicium* (family name) of which Julius, Claudius and Flavius are common examples among provincials of the early imperial period; third, a *cognomen* (surname), often reflecting local or regional characteristics. Officers in auxiliary units will have possessed Roman citizenship but ordinary recruits to these units did not officially receive it until their discharge. Although not strictly entitled to do so, such auxiliary soldiers did sometimes adopt the *tria nomina* before discharge.

Military and administrative terms

In the fort

Praetorium: the residential complex housing the commanding officer and his household.

Principia: the official headquarters complex at the centre of the fort.

Via principalis: the street forming the central longitudinal axis of the camp.

Types of unit and their subdivisions

Ala quingenaria: an auxiliary cavalry unit with a nominal strength of 500 men.

Ala milliaria: an auxiliary cavalry unit with a nominal strength of 1000 men.

Cohors: the main subdivision of the legion; each legion had 10 cohorts with a nominal strength of 500, except for the First Cohort which had 800.

Cohors quingenaria peditata: an auxiliary infantry regiment with a nominal strength of 500.

Cohors quingenaria equitata: a part-mounted regiment with a nominal strength of 500, of which 120 were cavalry.

Cohors milliaria peditata: an infantry regiment with a nominal strength of 1000.
Cohors milliaria equitata: a part-mounted regiment with a nominal strength of 1000, of which 240 were cavalry.
Centuria: the main infantry subdivision of the cohort, containing 80 men, further subdivided into 10 sections (*contubernia*). There were 6 centuries in a *cohors quingenaria* and 10 in a *cohors milliaria*; the numbers of men in each century may have been reduced in the part-mounted cohorts, allowing for the extra cavalry.
Turma: the main subdivision of an *ala* and of the cavalry contingent in a *cohors equitata*, probably consisting of 32 cavalrymen.

Personnel

Legatus Augusti or *consularis*: the title of the provincial governor of Britain (and of the other provinces to which the emperor made direct appointments) was *legatus Augustus pro praetore*. The governor of Britain was always a person who had held the consulship and the term *consularis* is frequently used as a slightly less formal term of reference.
Legatus legionis: the commander of a legion, a man of senatorial status normally with the rank of ex-quaestor or ex-praetor (two of the magistracies in the senatorial career held before the consulship, normally at the ages of about 25 and 30 respectively).
Centurio regionarius: a centurion, normally from a legion, appointed to the military and administrative supervision of a particular geographical area.
Praefectus cohortis: the equestrian officer in command of an auxiliary cohort. Quingenary cohorts were commanded by *praefecti*; milliary cohorts were normally commanded by *tribuni* but the Tungrian cohorts seem exceptionally to have had *praefecti* in command.
Beneficiarius: an adjutant seconded for special duties to a higher-ranking officer. Those most commonly found with this title are adjutants of the provincial governor (*beneficiarii consularis*) but *praefecti* of auxiliary cohorts and *legati legionis* also had them.
Centurio: the officer in command of a *centuria* of infantrymen.
Decurio: the officer in command of a *turma* of cavalrymen.
Optio: the second-in-command or deputy centurion in a *centuria* of infantrymen.
Principalis: a military rank in which were grouped a number of posts, junior and senior staff officers, *optiones*, standard-bearers etc.; holders of these

posts received either double the basic pay (*duplicarius*) or pay-and-a-half (*sesquiplicarius*).

Duplicarius: an officer receiving double the basic pay; the term is sometimes used to designate the second-in-command in a century or a *turma*.

Miscellaneous

Diploma: a certificate granted to an auxiliary soldier normally when he received an honorable discharge after 25 years of service. The certificate recorded the grant of discharge (*honesta missio*) and the privileges attaching to the veteran's status, principally the Roman citizenship and the right to contract a legally valid marriage.

Eques Romanus: a member of the *ordo equester*, the second highest status and property class in the Roman social order. The property qualification required for membership of the equestrian class was 400,000 sesterces, compared to 1 million for membership of the senatorial order.

Coins, weights and measures

For detailed calculations see Duncan-Jones (1982), 369–72.

Denarius: the basic denomination in the Roman currency system, a silver coin with an admixture of bronze, struck at 1/96 of a pound at this period. The basic pay of the Roman soldier was 300 *denarii* a year.

Sestertius: a coin worth one-quarter of the *denarius*.

As: a coin worth one-quarter of the *sestertius*, or one-sixteenth of the *denarius*.

Libra: a Roman pound, approximately 323 grams.

Modius: the so-called Italic *modius*, of approximately 8.62 litres, was the most commonly used measure of capacity and in the Vindolanda texts it occurs as a measure for liquid and dry goods.

Sextarius: one-sixteenth of a *modius*, approximately 0.539 litres.

APPENDIX II

THE TEXTS

This Appendix contains a selection of the most substantial and important of the writing-tablets. Extensive notes on matters of interpretation, palaeography and historical detail will be found in the editions in *Tab. Vindol.* II. For discussion of the many points of linguistic interest see also Adams (1994).

It should be noted that the line numeration is continuous in texts which are complete; in incomplete texts each column and any text on the back of the tablets is numbered separately. Unless otherwise noted the text is written along the grain of the wood; the symbol ↓ indicates that the text is written across the grain of the wood. In addition, the following conventions are employed in the presentation of the texts:

i, ii: designate separate columns of text following the original layout.
. . .: indicates that the text is broken or incomplete at the top or bottom.
m^1, *m^2*: distinguish different hands in the text.
[ ]: indicates a lacuna in the text.
[*c.4*]: estimate of the number of letters missing in a lacuna.
uacat: a space left by the scribe on the tablet.
⟦abc⟧: letters crossed out or erased by the scribe.
⌞abc⌟: letters or words added by the scribe above the line.
<abc>: letters erroneously omitted by the scribe.
{abc}: superfluous letters written by the scribe.
. . . : represents traces of letters visible on the tablet which have been left unread.
ạḅc̣: doubtful or partially preserved letters.
praef(ecto), *(centurio)*: expansion or resolution of an abbreviation or symbol.

Documents, accounts and lists

1. Strength report of the First Cohort of Tungrians (*Tab. Vindol.* I 154)

PLATE IV

↓ xv K(alendas) Ịuṇịas n(umerus) p(urus) [co]ḥ(ortis) ị
Tụngrọ-
ṛuṃ cui prae<e>st Iulius Vere-
c̣ụndus praef(ectus) dc̣c̣lịị in is (centuriones) vi
ẹx ẹis absentes
singulares leg̣(ati) xlvi
officio F̣ẹrocis
Coris c̣c̣cxxxvịị
ịn is (centuriones) iị
Londinio (centurio) [i]
uạṣ..aḍ[*c.4*]...ap̣aḍụṇ... vi
in is (centurio) i
]ạc̣.........aḷlia viiii
in is (centurio) i
...c...ip̣ẹndiaṭuṃ xi
]ịṇ.ạ ị
xxxxv
ṣụṃma absentes cccclṿị
in is (centuriones) v
reliqui praesenṭes cclxxx̣x̣ṿị
in is (centurio) i
ẹx eis
aegri xv
uolnerati vi
ḷịp̣pientes [x]
summa eoṛ[um] x̣xxi
reliqui ualent[es cc]lx̣ṿ
in [is (centurio) i]

18 May, net number of the First Cohort of Tungrians, of which the commander is Iulius Verecundus the prefect, 752, including 6 centurions.
Of whom there are absent:
guards of the governor 46
at the office of Ferox

at Coria		337
	including (?) 2 centurions	
at London	(?) a centurion	
. . .		6
	including 1 centurion	
. . .		9
	including 1 centurion	
. . .		11
at (?) . . .		(?) 1
		45
total absentees		456
	including 5 centurions	
remainder, present		296
	including 1 centurion	
from these:		
sick		15
wounded		6
suffering from inflammation of the eyes		10
total of these		31
remainder, fit for active service		265
	including 1 centurion.	

6 Ferox was evidently a high-ranking officer, perhaps the commander of the Ninth Legion (Hispana), based at York.

7 Coria, a name which occurs several times in the Vindolanda tablets, seems certain to be the Roman name of Corbridge (hitherto believed to be 'Coriosopitum' or something similar).

12–16 These lines contain details of small groups of soldiers absent on various duties or at other places but the writing is too abraded to be legible.

2. Report of work assignments (*Tab. Vindol.* II 155)

vii K(alendas) Maịạs f̣ạbṛicis h(omines) cccxxxxiii
ex eịṣ suṭores *uacat* xii
ṣ[tr]ụctọṛẹṣ ad balṇeum xviii
[a]d plumbụm *uacat* [
[a]ḍ . aṛ.[
.[..]..a[ ]ụaletudinar[
ad furnaceṣ [

ad lutum [
tectores [
...apil.[
ạḍ cae[
[.]..b[
ad p.[
cum[
. . . .

25 April, in the workshops, 343 men.
of these: shoemakers, 12
builders to the bath-house 18
for lead . . .
for . . . wagons (?) . . .
. . . hospital . . .
to the kilns . . .
for clay . . .
plasterers . . .
for . . . tents (?) . . .
for rubble . . .
. . .

5 Probably a reference to *carros* or the diminutive form *carrula* (see *Tab. Vindol.* II 315.2 note).

10 This should perhaps be read as a reference to *papiliones*.

3. Memorandum (?) about the Britons (*Tab. Vindol.* II 164) PLATE V

. . . .
↓ nenụ...[.]n. Brittoneṣ
nimium multi · equites
gladis · non ụtụṇtur equites · nec residunt
Brittunculi · ụt · iaculos
mittant

. . . the Britons are unprotected by armour(?). There are very many cavalry. The cavalry do not use swords nor do the wretched Britons mount in order to throw javelins.

1 The suggested restoration is: *ne nụḍị ṣ[i]nṭ* or *ṣ[u]nṭ*.

4. Military report (*Tab. Vindol.* II 127)

]. Iụ [
[renunti]ụṃ cḥọṛtis viiii
[Batauor]ụṃ ọṃṇes ad loca
[q(ui) uideb]uṇṭ et inpedimenta .ṛ
] *uacat*
[*vacat*? renu]ṇṭịạuẹrunt optiones
[et] cuṛạṭọṛẹṣ *uacat*
[detul]ịṭ Verecundus opṭịọ
[*c*.5] ....

(Date). Report of the Ninth Cohort of Batavians. All are at their posts and they will also see to the baggage (which is present?). The *optiones* and *curatores* made the report. Verecundus the *optio* . . . delivered it.

1 The month name is probably June, in which case the date will be in the second half of May or the first half of June, depending on whether it was preceded by the Kalends, the Ides or the Nones; for the form of recording the date see **2**.1.

4 The word to be supplied at the end of the line is perhaps *praesentia*.

6–7 The *optiones* are second in the command in the centuries of the cohort. The term *curator* probably denotes a specific function or task rather than a regular rank.

9 This line will have contained the sickle-shaped centurial symbol and the name of Verecundus' century, probably 'century of Crescens'.

5. Requests for leave (*Tab. Vindol.* II 174 and 175)

(α) ṛ[ogo
dig̣[num me habeas
cui des commeatum
Ụḷucịo *uacat*
uacat

. . . I ask . . . that you consider me a worthy person to whom to grant leave at Ulucium (?).

4 Ulucium must be a place, but it cannot be identified.

(β) .....[.] ḥạ[b]eas · cui ·
des · commeatum
Córis Messicus t[..
rógo · domine [
. . . .
Back:]Ṃessic̣.

I, Messicus . . ., ask, my lord, that you consider me a worthy person to whom to grant leave at Coria. (Back) . . . of (?) Messicus.

3 For Coria see **1**.7 note.

6. Account of wheat (*Tab. Vindol.* II 180)

↓ ratio frumenti eṃ[ensi ex quo
ipse dedi in cupaṃ [
mihi ad panem [
Macrino m(odii) vii
Felicio Victori iussu Sp̣ẹctati
comodati m(odii) xxvi
in follibus tribus patri ṃ(odii) xix
Macrino m(odii) xiii
bubulcaris in siluam m(odii) viii
item Amabili ad fanum m(odii) iii
[..]. Idus Septem(bres) Crescenti
iussu .[.]..ị m(odii) iii
item . [*c.6*]ẹ[ ]..
Macṛ[..]..us.[ ]. ṃ(odii) x̣ṿ ..
item ma.[*c.6*] m(odii) [ ]iii
patri ad [*c.6*].as m(odii) ii
vi Kal(endas) [O]c̣toḅṛ[es
Lu[..].[.. ben]ẹficịạr[io] m(odii) vi
Felicio Victori m(odii) xv
ad turṭas tibi m(odii) ii
Crescenti m(odii) ix
militibus legionaribus
iussu Firmi m(odii) xi[
Candido m(odii) [
tibi in folle br.gẹse [
tibi [
Lucconi ad porcos [
Primo Luci [
tibi [
Lucconi in ussus suos [
item [..]ụọs m[.]..ị.[
in [.]uọtur[.].

patri [a]d ị[uu]ẹncoṣ [
item inter metrum [
libr.s xv redd.   librạẹ xv[
fiunt   m(odii) [
item mihi ad panem m(odii) i[
summạ f̣ṛumẹnṭị   m(odii) cccx̣x̣ ṣ(emis)

Account of wheat measured out from that which
I myself have put into the barrel:
to myself, for bread . . .
to Macrinus, *modii* 7
to Felicius Victor on the order of Spectatus
provided as a loan (?), *modii* 26
in three sacks, to father, *modii* 19
to Macrinus, *modii* 13
to the oxherds at the wood, *modii* 8
likewise to Amabilis at the shrine, *modii* 3
. . . September . ., to Crescens
on the order of Firmus (?), *modii* 3
likewise . . ., *modii* . .
to Macr. . . . . ., *modii* (?) 15
likewise to Ma. . . (?), *modii* . .
to father . . ., *modii* 2
26 September
to Lu. . . the *beneficiarius*, *modii* 6
to Felicius Victor, *modii* 15
for twisted loaves (?), to you, *modii* 2
to Crescens, *modii* 9
to the legionary soldiers
on the order of Firmus, *modii* 11+
to Candidus, *modii* . .
to you, in a sack from Briga (?), . . .
to you, . . .
to Lucco, in charge of the pigs . . .
to Primus, slave (?) of Lucius . . .
to you . . .
to Lucco for his own use . . .
likewise that which I have sent . . . *modii* . . (?)

in the century of Voturius (?)
to father, in charge of the oxen . . .
likewise, within the measure . . . (?)
15 pounds yield 15+ pounds (?) . . .
total, *modii* . . .
likewise to myself, for bread, *modii* . .
total of wheat, *modii* 320½.

5 The names Spectatus, Firmus (line 23) and Candidus (line 24) also occur in **32**, a letter which was found in close proximity to this account.

18 This must be a reference to the *beneficiarius* of the prefect of the cohort, an officer attached to the commander for special duties; the reference in **33**.i.10 is probably to the same person.

25 The word appears to be *brigense* but its meaning is very uncertain. For the place-name Briga see **10**.38 and **22**.c.v.2.

34 The meaning of the phrase *inter metrum* is obscure. It might be taken with the following line, indicating that 'on average' so many pounds of cereal will make so many pounds of bread.

7. Account of receipts and debts (*Tab. Vindol.* II 181)

. . . .
↓].ndi .[*c.6*]ṛ..
uacat?
.ṣ..[.C]andid. (ḍẹṇạṛịọṣ) ịị
lịgnis emtis (ḍẹṇạṛịọṣ) ṿiị
sticam (ḍẹṇạṛịọṣ) ịịi
ab Tetrico [(denarios)] .
ab Primo (ḍẹṇạṛịọṣ) ịị ṣ(emissem)
ab Alione ueterinario (ḍẹṇạṛịọṣ) x.
ab Vitale balniatore (ḍẹṇạṛịọṣ) ịịi
summa (denarii) xxxiiii s(emis)
reliqui debent
Ingenus (denarios) vii
Acranius (denarios) iii
equites Vardulli (denarios) vii
contubernalis Tagamatịṣ
ụexṣịllari (denarios) iii
summa (denarii) xx

. . .
. . . Candidus, *denarii* 2 (?)
for timbers purchased, *denarii* 7 (?)
a tunic, *denarii* 3 (?)
from Tetricus, *denarii* . .
from Primus, *denarii* 2½ (?)
from Alio the veterinary doctor, *denarii* 10+
from Vitalis the bathman, *denarii* 3 (?)
total, *denarii* 34½
the rest owe:
Ingenuus, *denarii* 7
Acranius, *denarii* 3
the Vardullian cavalrymen, *denarii* 7
the companion of Tagamatis (?) the flag-bearer, *denarii* 3
total, *denarii* 20.

8. Account of sums received (*Tab. Vindol.* II 182) PLATE V

i
[*c.5* ⟦c]ọrnicen pretio
[*c.4*]ṣ m(odiorum) xv (denarios) xii (assem i) (semissem) (quadrantem)⟧
re]ḅus minutis (denarios) ii (asses ii)
⟦Sabinus Trever (denarios) xxiix s(emissem) (asses ii)⟧
Ịrc̣ucisso ex pretio lardi (denarios) xiii s(emissem)
Felicio (centurio) lardi p(ondo) xxxxv
item lardi pernam p(ondo) xv s(emissem)
f̣ịun{n}t p(ondo) lx s(emissem) (denarios) viii
(asses ii)
item accipi ̣ reb<us> miṇuṭis (denarios) vi
(asses ii) s(emissem) (q̣ụạḍṛạṇṭẹṃ)
ii
Vattus [
⟦Victor ua ̣[⟧
⟦pretio caballi [⟧
⟦Exomnius (centurio) (denarios) [⟧
Atrectus ceruesar[ius
ex pretio ferri (denarios) i[
pretio exungiae (denarios) xi (asses ii)

Andecarus (denarios) *uacat*
Sanctus (denarios) *uacat*

⟦. . . , bugler, for the price of
. . . *modii* 15, *denarii* 12, *asses* 1¾⟧
likewise, for sundries, *denarii* 2, *asses* 2
⟦Sabinus from Trier, *denarii* 38½, *asses* 2⟧
Ircucisso, as part of the price of bacon, *denarii* 13½
Felicio the centurion, bacon, 45 pounds
likewise, bacon-lard, 15½ pounds
total, 60½ pounds, *denarii* 8, *asses* 2 . .
likewise, he has (?) received for sundries *denarii* 6,
asses 2¾
Vattus . . .
⟦Victor . . .⟧
⟦For the price of a horse . . .⟧
⟦Exomnius the centurion, *denarii* . . .⟧
Atrectus the brewer,
as part of the price of iron, *denarii* . .
for the price of pork-fat, *denarii* 11, *asses* 2
Andecarus, *denarii*
Sanctus, *denarii.*

i.2 The symbol at the end of the line (also in line 9) is a fraction of an *as*, probably a quarter.

5 The name *Ircucisso* has not previously been attested.

9. Account of miscellaneous goods (*Tab. Vindol.* II 184) PLATE VI

i
(centuria) Uceṇi
|– superarias (denarios) xiii.[
|– Tagarminis ⟦.⟧
|– piper (denarios) ii
C̣ambax Tapponis
ṣ[udari]ụṃ (denarios) ii
].mni..[.].ubar[
|– ampullam [
.ụṛịọ Ṣṭ..ọnis
|– sudarium (denarios) ii

– Ammius [
]xxiix
].i
]ṃ (denarios) iii (asses ii) (quadrantem)
].s
]..i (denarios) i s(emissem) (assem i)
].armal *traces?*
ii
coturnum (denarios) iii ṣ(emissem)
Messor ⟦.......⟧
– sagaciam (denarios) v (asses iii)
Luc̣ius scutarius
sebum (denarios) [
U]xperus
]ị[
Agị.[
ṣ[
Huep..[
sudạṛ[ ] (denarios) ii
Tullio Carp̣ẹnṭạri
uacat of 2 lines
(denarios) xḷ *traces*
iii
(centuria) Tullionis
corrigia (denarios) ii s(emissem)
– sebum (denarios) ii
sudari(um) (denarium) i
Butimas
sebum (denarios) ii[
d sudar(ium) (denarios) .[
]o. subạrṃalọ
sebum (denarios) [
C]aleḍus
uacat
uell[*c.8*]........
ue.[*c.8*].aliator

(i. 1–11)
Century of Ucen(i)us (?)
overcoats, *denarii* 13+
Tagarminis
pepper, *denarii* 2
Gambax son of Tappo
towel, *denarii* 2,
Sollemnis (?) . . .
a flask . . .
Furio (?) son of Stipo (?)
towel, *denarii* 2
Ammius . . .
. . .
(ii. 19–iii. 40)
buskin, *denarii* 3½
Messor
a cloak, *denarii* 5, *asses* 3
Lucius the shield-maker
tallow, *denarii* . .
. . . Uxperus.
. . .
Agilis (?)
tallow (?), . . .
Huep . . .
towel, *denarii* 2
Tullio son of Carpentarius
. . . *denarii* 40+
century of Tullio:
thongs, *denarii* 2½
tallow, *denarii* 2
towel (?), *denarius* 1
Butimas
tallow, *denarii* 2+
towel, *denarii* . .
. . .
tallow (?), *denarii* 2½.
Caledus

i — There are check marks at the left of several of the entries in this account, but their significance is not clear. The items or commodities appear to precede the names of the persons to whom they are accounted.

ii.18 — The singular *coturnum* is probably used collectively for a pair of boots, perhaps of a rustic type.

iii.42–3 — The reading and the meaning of these lines, which are written upside down in relation to the main text, are unclear.

10. Account of money and foodstuffs (*Tab. Vindol.* II 190)

. . . .

a]ḍ sacrum (denarios) [
]ṃ ạḍ sacrum (ḍẹṇạṛịọṣ) [
]ạtaṃ ad sacrum [
uacat
m²? xiii K(alendas) Iuḷi[as
hordẹ[i
ceruesạ[e
x̣[ii] K(alendas) Iuliạṣ
hordei m(odios) iiii [
çeruesae m(odios) ii
[xi K(alendas) Iu]ḷias hordei [
].m ad hoṛ[
].tum
]ṃ(odios) ii
x K(alendas) Iulias
hordei m(odios) v s(emissem)
allatus ụini ..ssec[
viiii K(alendas) Iulias
hordei m(odios) v s(emissem)
uini m(odium) i (sextarios) xiiii
ceruesae m(odios) iii
viii K(alendas) Iulias
hordei m(odios) vị.[
çẹṛụẹṣạẹ m(odios) iii (sextarios) ...
uini m(odium) i (sextarios) xii
aceti (sextarios) ii

per Priuatum
muriae (sextarium) i s(emissem)
per P̣riuatum
axungiae (ṣẹx̣ṭạṛịọṣ) x mut[(uo)
domino ad stipes
per Priuatum
uini m(odium) i ad saç̣ṛụṃ
d<i>uae
uini (sextarios) xii
per Priuaṭụ[m
vii K(alendas) Iuḷias
hordei (sextarios) .ị.
domịni Brigae ṃạṇ[se-
runt
uacat

. . . for the festival, *denarii* . .
. . . for the festival, *denarii* . .
. . . for the festival . . .
19 June
of barley . . .
of Celtic beer . . .
20 June:
of barley, *modii* 4+ (?)
of Celtic beer, *modii* 2
21 June, of barley . . .
. . . to the granary (?) . . .
. . .
. . . *modii* 2
22 June
of barley, *modii* 5½ (?)
Allatus (?), of Massic wine (?) . . .
23 June
of barley, *modii* 5½
of wine, *modius* 1 *sextarii* 14
of Celtic beer, *modii* 3
24 June
of barley, *modii* 6+

of Celtic beer, *modii* 3 *sextarii* . .
of wine, *modius* 1 *sextarii* 12
of sour wine, *sextarii* 2
through Privatus
of fish-sauce, *sextarii* 1½
through Privatus
of pork-fat, *sextarii* 10 as a loan (?)
to the lord for charitable donations
through Privatus
of wine, *modius* 1 for the festival
of the goddess (?)
of wine, *sextarii* 12
through Privatus
25 June
of barley, *sextarii* 11½ (?)
the lords have remained at Briga.

1–3 These lines may belong to a different account (or part of the account) from what follows.

16 This may be a reference to Massic wine, an Italian vintage of high reputation.

26 Privatus is a personal name and must belong to a slave in the commanding officer's household.

38–9 Briga is a place-name but it cannot be identified. See also **22**.c.v.2.

11. Account of meat and other foodstuffs (*Tab. Vindol.* II 191)

. . . ̣ . . . .
↓]in p[
]ṣ (denarios) [
condimen[t-
capream [
salis .[
porcellum [
pernam. [
in p[
frumen[ti
ceruin[am
in p. [
ad condiṭ[

caprea[
⟦s(umma) (denarii) [⟧
m^{2}? s(umma) (denarii) xx [
m^{1} braciṣ .[
(denarios) ị[
.ụm[

. . . in
. . . *denarii* . . .
spices . . .
roe-deer . . .
of salt . . .
young pig . . .
ham . . .
in . . .
of wheat . . .
venison . . .
in . . .
for pickling (?)
roe-deer . . .
⟦total, *denarii* . . .⟧
total, *denarii* 20+
of emmer . . .
denarii
total (?) . . .

1 This should perhaps be restored as *in p[raetorio* (i.e. in the commanding-officer's residence); see also lines 8 and 11.

16 *bracis* was a cereal used in the brewing of beer (see **10**); the precise type is uncertain.

12. Account of foodstuffs and textiles (*Tab. Vindol.* II 192)

↓ ạ Ḉauuone
bedocem (ḍẹṇạṛịọṣ) [
fabae m(odios) .v (ḍẹṇạṛịọṣ) [
lanae p(ondo) xxxiix[
p(ondo) . (ḍẹṇạṛịọṣ) xiị s(emissem) (assem i) [
ṭosseas iii [
mellis m(odios) [
sagum [

s(umma) ⟦(denarii) lxx[]⟧
(denarii) [
Back: ratio Gauonis

From Gavo:
a coverlet (?) [*dẹnarii*]
of beans, *modii* 55 (?), *ḍenarii* . .
of wool, 38 lbs
. . lbs *denarii* 12½, *as* 1
bedspreads, 3 [*denarii* . .]
of honey, *modii* . . [*dẹnarii* . .]
a *sagum* [*denarii* . .]
totaḷ: ⟦*denarii* 70+⟧
denarii . .
(Back) Account of Gavo.

1 It is not known who or where Gavo was; there is another account of Gavo including items of clothing (*Tab. Vindol.* II 207). In both his accounts the name is spelled differently on the front and back.

8 A *sagum* is a type of cloak. There are several different Latin terms for cloaks in the Vindolanda tablets (see also **14**, **20**). Since the precise differences between them are obscure or unknown, they are not translated.

13. List of household equipment (*Tab. Vindol.* II 194)

A. . . . .
↓ .[
scuṭụḷ[as] ịị[
paropsiḍeṣ [ ] ṿ⟦ii⟧
acetabuḷ[a]iii
ouaria · ịii
in laterar[..].
lanceṃ
scutul[a]ṃ
B. ↑ compenḍ[iá]rium et
lucerṇ[am] ạeneam
panaria · [ ]iiii
calices · [ ]ii ·
in ṭhẹ[ca]
trullas · [ ] theca

s[
.[
. . . .

(A) . . .
shallow dishes, 2 (?)
side-plates, 5 (?)
vinegar-bowls, 3 (?)
egg-cups, 3
on the purlin (?)
a platter
a shallow dish
(B) a strong-box (?) and a bronze lamp
bread-baskets, 4 (?)
cups, 2 (?)
in a box
bowls, 2 (?) in a box . . .

The tablet contains text on both sides. The sides are designated as A and B but the order in which they should be read is uncertain.

A.6 This might mean that the items following were stored or located on a beam in the kitchen.

14. List of household goods and clothing (*Tab. Vindol.* II 196)

↓ cubitoṛ[a
lodicum · pạ[r
paenulas · caṇ[
de synthesi · [
paenulas · e.[
et laenam · e[t
cenatoriạ[
sunthesi[
subpaenụ[l
ḷiạ.[
subuclas · b[
á Ṭrạnqụ[illo
subpaenu[l
⟦á Ṭraṇqụịḷḷ[o]⟧

á Brocchó [
tunicas · im[
simicị.[
tunicas · cẹn[

for dining
pair(s) of blankets . . .
paenulae, white (?) . . .
from an outfit:
paenulae . . .
and a *laena* and a (?) . . .
for dining
loose robe(s) . . .
under-*paenula(e)* . . .
vests . . .
from Tranquillus:
under-*paenula(e)* . . .
⟦from Tranquillus⟧
from Brocchus:
tunics . . .
half-belted (?) . . .
tunics for dining (?) . . .

3 No attempt is made to translate the different terms for types of cloaks, see **11**.8 note.
12 Tranquillus does not appear elsewhere in the tablets.
15 Brocchus may be the person who appears as a correspondent of Flavius Cerialis (see **16**, **18**) but the name is reasonably common.

There are five incomplete lines on the back of the leaf listing a lamp with a handle (*catacysen ansatam*), rings (*anulos*) and perhaps cushions (*ceruicalia*).

Letters

15. Draft letter from Flavius Cerialis to Crispinus (*Tab. Vindol.* II 225)

[ ] *uacat* Crispino suo [*uacat?*
[G]ṛattịo Çrisp̣ino redeunte .[...
[*c.10*] ⟦non fui mihi⟧ et .ḍ. [..
[*c.7* li]benter amplexụṣ ṣ[um do-
ṃine ṣạlutandi te oc̣c̣ạṣṣịọṇẹṃ
[d]ọminum meum et quem saluom
⟦ḥạbere⟧ esse et omnis spei

⟦suae⟧ compotem inter praecipuạ
uoti habeo hoc enim de
me semper meruisti usque
ad hanc ḍ[*c.4*].tem cuius f̣ịḍ-
ục̣ịạ họ[*c.6*]e te primuṃ [...
[*c.4*]..[*c.6*]..⌞ut⌟ẹ.il[...
Back: [....]m Marcẹllum clarissị[mum ui-
[rum] consularem meum quar.[....
[oc]c̣assionem nunc ut.[*c.11*
[...]. ṭibi amicorum dọ[*c.10*
sụạ [p]ṛạẹsentia quos tụ[*c.9*
illius scio plurimos haberẹ [....
quomodo uoḷes imple quidq̣[uid
de te exspecto et me .ḷụ. [.]...
aṃicis ita instrue ut beneficio
tuo militiam [po]ṣṣim iucundam
experiri ha[ec ti]bi a Vindolanda scribo .[*c.6*]. hibernạ [..
[.].ṇ.ụ. ḥ..[*c.6*].ius a.[
. . . .

To his Crispinus. Since Grattius Crispinus is returning to . . . and . . . I have gladly seized the opportunity, my lord, of greeting you, you who are my lord and the man whom it is my very special wish to be in good health and master of all your hopes. For you have always deserved this of me right up to the present high office (?). In reliance on this . . . you first . . . greet (?) . . . Marcellus, that most distinguished man, my governor. He therefore offers (?) the opportunity now of . . . the talents (?) of your friends through his presence, of which you have, I know, very many, thanks to him (?). Now, in whatever way you wish, fulfil what I expect of you and . . . so furnish me with very many friends that thanks to you I may be able to enjoy a pleasant period of military service. I write this to you from Vindolanda where my winter-quarters are (?)

1 The identity and position of Crispinus are unknown but the tone and content of the letter suggest that he was probably highly-placed and influential. The Crispinus named in line 2 must be a different person (the name is very common).

16. Copy of a letter from Flavius Cerialis to Brocchus (*Tab. Vindol.* II 233)

i

Flauius Cerialis Broccho
suo salutem
si me amas frater rogo
ṃittas mihi plagas
].[
. . . .

ii

fortissime *uacat*
frusta exeṛc̣ịas
uacat

Flavius Cerialis to his Brocchus, greetings. If you love me, brother, I ask that you send me some hunting-nets (?) . . . you should repair the pieces very strongly.

ii.2 This is probably a form of the verb *exsarcio*. The reading of these lines is complicated by the fact that there are the remains of an account or list of foodstuffs (including pigs' trotters, *ungellae*) written across the grain in this part of the tablet.

17. Copy of a letter from Flavius Cerialis to September (*Tab. Vindol.* II 234)

i

Flauius Cerialis Septembri
suo saluṭeḿ
quod uis domine c̣ṛaṣ
id eṣṭ ịịị Ṇọṇas Ọc̣[t]ó-
bres merc.. p̣ạ..[

ii

qui f̣ẹṛạmụṣ ṭẹṃ-
pestates ⟦et hiem⟧ ⌞etiam⌟ si
molestae sint

Flavius Cerialis to his September, greetings. Tomorrow, which is 5 October, as you wish my lord, I will provide some goods (?) . . . by means of which (?) we may endure the storms even if they are troublesome.

i.5 The suggested reading and restoration is *mercẹṃ paṛạ[bo.*

ii.2 *et hiem* is crossed out and *etiam* is inserted above the line. In view of the similarity of the sound this must be a dictation error.

18. Letter from Niger and Brocchus to Flavius Cerialis (*Tab. Vindol.* II 248)

i

Niger et Brocchus Çeriạḷị
suo salutem'
óptamus frater it quot
acturus es felicis-
simum sit erit autem
quom et uotis nostris

ii

conueniat hoc
pro te precari et tú
sis dignissimus con-
sulari n(ostro) utique mạ-
turius occurres
*m*² op<t>amus frater
bene ualẹrẹ tẹ
domine *traces* ṇọ. ẹxṣpẹç
Back: *m*¹ [Fl]ạụ[io] Cerịạḷ[i
[prae]f̣(ecto) coḥ(ortis)
traces?

Niger and Brocchus to their Cerialis, greeting. We pray, brother, that what you are about to do will be most successful. It will be so, indeed, since it is both in accord with our wishes to make this prayer on your behalf and you yourself are most worthy. You will assuredly meet our governor quite soon. (2nd hand) We pray, our lord and brother, that you are in good health . . . expect . . . (?). (Back, 1st hand) To Flavius Cerialis, prefect of the cohort . . .

i.1 This person is probably not Oppius Niger (see **23**). He may well be Valerius Niger who is mentioned in another tablet (*Tab. Vindol.* II 465).

ii.14 Possibly the writer intended the imperative *exspecta* following *nos* and suggesting the prospect of a visit to Cerialis.

19. Letter of recommendation to Flavius Cerialis (*Tab. Vindol.* II 250)

i

[*c.4*]ịus Karuṣ Ç[e]ṛ[iali

[su]ọ *uacat* ṣ[alutem
[*c.4*]brigionus petiṭ a ṃẹ
[domi]ne ut eum tibi coṃ-
meṇdareṭ rogo ergo do-
miṇẹ ṣị quod a te petieriṭ
[u]ẹḷịṣ ẹi subscribere
Anniọ Ẹquesṭri (centurioni) ṛegi-
onarịo Luguualio ro-
go ut eum commen-
ii
[*c.4*] ḍigneriṣ .[...
[...].que nom[ine
ḍebetorem m[e tibi
obligaturus ọp̣[to
te felicissimum
bene ⟦f⟧ụạḷẹṛẹ
uacat
m^2 uale frater
Back:m^1 [C]ẹriali
praẹf̣(ecto)

. . .ius Karus to his Cerialis, greetings. . . . Brigionus (?) has requested me, my lord, to recommend him to you. I therefore ask, my lord, if you would be willing to support him in what he has requested of you. I ask that you think fit to commend him to Annius Equester, centurion in charge of the region, at Luguvalium, by doing which you will place me in debt to you both in his name (?) and my own (?). I pray that you are enjoying the best of fortune and are in good health. (2nd hand) Farewell, brother. (Back, 1st hand) To Cerialis, prefect.

i.2 As is normal, the word *salutem* is justified at the right but it is very unusual to find *suo* justified at the left.

20. Letter from Clodius (?) Super to Flavius Cerialis (*Tab. Vindol.* II 255)

i
[Cl]ọdius Super Ceriali suo
salutem
[V]alentinum n(ostrum) a Ḉallia reuer-

sum commode uestem adprobas-
se gratulatus sum per quem
te saluto et rogo ut ea quae
ussibus puerorum meorum
opus sunt mittas mihi sa-

ii

gaçias ṣex̣ sagạ [*c.3* pallio-]
ḷa septem tu[nicas se]x̣
qụạe scis çerte hịc me ṇọ[n
ṛịṭe impetrare çum simụṣ
nonạ.cusi etiam aḍ ẹọ[rum
traṇslationem *m²* uạḷẹạṣ
domine frater
çarissiṃẹ ẹṭ[*c.8*]ṣ
ṣiṃẹ *traces?*

Back:*m¹?* Flauió Ceria-
li praef(ecto)
ạ [C]ḷ[o]ḍio Supeṛọ (centurione)

Clodius Super to his Cerialis, greetings. I was pleased that our friend Valentinus on his return from Gaul has duly approved the clothing. Through him I greet you and ask that you send the things which I need for the use of my boys, that is, six *sagaciae*, n *saga*, seven *palliola*, six (?) tunics, which you well know I cannot properly get hold of here, since we are . . . ready (?) for the boys' transfer (?). (2nd hand) May you fare well, my dearest lord and brother, and . . . (Back, 1st hand) To Flavius Cerialis, prefect, from Clodius Super, centurion.

i. 1 Super was perhaps a legionary centurion. The tone of his letter to the auxiliary prefect suggests that he was perhaps of equivalent social standing, i.e. a member of the equestrian class.

i. 3 Apart from a reference to Rome (*Tab. Vindol.* II 283.4) this is the only certain mention in the writing-tablets of a place outside Britain (although there are several unknown place-names some of which might be in Gaul).

7 The *pueri* are likely to be slaves of Super (the word is also used, probably with the same meaning, in *Tab. Vindol.* II 260.7).

ii. 12–14 The reading and interpretation of this passage have not been satisfactorily explained.

21. Birthday invitation of Claudia Severa to Sulpicia Lepidina (*Tab. Vindol.* II 291) PLATE VI

i

Cl(audia) · Seuerá Lepidinae [suae
[sa]ḷ[u]ṭẹm
iii Idus Septembṛ[e]ṣ soror ad dieṃ'
sollemnem ṇatalem meum rogó
libenter f̣aciás ut uenias
ad nos iụcundiorem mihi

ii

[diem] interuentú tuo facturá si
[.].[*c.3*]ṣ *uacat*
Cerial[em t]ụum salutá Aelius meus .[
et filioḷụs ṣalutant *uacat*
m_2 *uacat* sperabo te soror
uale soroṛ anima
mea ita ụạḷeam
karissima ẹt haue
Back: m^1 Sulpiciae Lep̣idinaẹ
Cerialịṣ
a S[e]ụerạ

Claudia Severa to her Lepidina greetings. On the third day before the Ides of September, sister, for the day of the celebration of my birthday, I give you a warm invitation to make sure that you come to us, to make the day more enjoyable for me by your arrival, if you are present (?). Give my greetings to your Cerialis. My Aelius and my little son send him (?) their greetings. (2nd hand) I shall expect you, sister. Farewell, sister, my dearest soul, as I hope to prosper, and hail. (Back, 1st hand) To Sulpicia Lepidina, (wife) of Cerialis, from Severa.

ii.7–8 The restoration suggested is *si / [a]d[eri]s* or *si / [tu] a[deri]s*.
Back.16–17 The word for 'wife' is omitted, as is not unusual.

22. Letter from Claudia Severa to Sulpicia Lepidina (*Tab. Vindol.* II 292)

a. i

. . . .

ṣạḷụṭẹṃ

ẹgo soror sicut tecum locuta fueram et promiseraṃ
ut peterem a Brocc̣hó et uenirem at te peti
et rẹṣ[po]ṇdit mihi <i>tạ corḍe semp[er li]c̣ịtum unạ́

b. ii

. . . .

traces

quomodocumque possim
at te peruenire sunt enim
necessariá quaedam qua[e]

iii

. . . .

traces?

rem meum epistuḷas ṃẹaṣ
accipies quibus scies quid
sim actura haec ṇọbiṣ

c. v

. . . .

traces

.ṛạ eram et Brigạe ṃansụṛạ
C̣erialem tuum a me saluta

uacat

b.Back: *m*[2] [ual]ẹ ṃ. ṣọror
ḳạrissima et aṇịṃạ
ma desideraṭissima
uacat *traces*

c.Back: *m*[1] Sulpic̣iaẹ Ḷẹpidị-
nae Ceriạ[li]ṣ *traces?*
a Seueṛạ Ḅ[rocchi

. . . greetings. Just as I had spoken with you, sister, and promised that I would ask Brocchus and would come to you, I asked him and he gave me the following reply, that it was always readily (?) permitted to me, together with . . . to come to you in whatever way I can. For there are certain essential things which . . . you will receive my letters by which you will know what I am going to do . . . I was . . . and will remain at Briga. Greet your Cerialis from me. (Back, 2nd hand) Farewell my sister, my dearest and most longed-for soul. (1st hand) To Sulpicia Lepidina, wife of Cerialis, from Severa, wife of Brocchus (?).

23. Letter from Oppius Niger to Priscinus (*Tab. Vindol.* II 295)

i

Oppius Niger Priscino [suo
ṣ[alutem
Crispum et .ẹ[*c.8*]ṣ ex̣ coh(orte)
·i· Tungrorum quos cum
epistulis ad consularem n(ostrum)
miseras a Bremetennaco

ii

].[..].[.]..[*c.3*
.[.].[.]..um Kal(endis) Ḟ[eb]ṛ[
m^2 ụale dọmịṇẹ
frateṛ
Back: (*traces of 2 lines*)

Oppius Niger to his Priscinus, greetings. Crispus and . . . from the 1st Cohort of Tungrians, whom you had sent with letters to our governor, [I have straightaway sent on (?)] from Bremetennacum to . . . on 1 February. (2nd hand) Farewell, my lord and brother.

i.3–4 For the First Cohort of Tungrians, see above **1**.

ii.8 A possible restoration is *a[d] L[i]ndum* (Lincoln). If the governor were at London, Ribchester to Lincoln would be a plausible part of the itinerary.

24. Letter to Lucius the decurion (*Tab. Vindol.* II 299)

i

. . . .
quod est principium epistulae
meae te fortem esse a Cordono-
uis amicus missit mihi ostria
quinquaginta quo uelocius fir-
. . . .

ii

].[*c.3*]ạṛ.....[
uacat
Back: Lucio decurion[i]
]..tẹṛi

. . . which is the principal reason for my letter (to express the wish?) that you are vigorous. A friend sent me fifty oysters from Cordonovi. In order that . . . more speedily . . . (Back) To Lucius, decurion from . . . (?).

i. 1–2 Cordonovi (or -vae, or perhaps -via) cannot be identified. Since it was a source of oysters, it might have been in the general area of the Thames estuary on the north Kent coast.

25. Letter from Severus to Candidus (*Tab. Vindol.* II 301)

i
Ṣ[eu]ẹṛ[u]ṣ Candido suo
salutem
sọuxtum saturnalicium
(asses) iiii aut sexs rogo frater
explices et radices ne minus (denarii) s(emissem)
ii
uacat
uale frater
uacat
Back: Candido Genialis
pṛạẹf̣(ecti)
a Seuero
...i ṣẹṛụọ

Severus to his Candidus, greetings. Regarding the . . for the Saturnalia, I ask you, brother, to see to them at a price of 4 or 6 asses and radishes to the value of not less than ½ *denarius*. Farewell, brother. (Back) To Candidus, slave of Genialis the prefect, from Severus, slave, of . . .

1 The reading of *sọuxtum* is clear but it is not a known Latin word and it is very difficult to see what could be meant. It is presumably some item connected with the celebration of the Saturnalia in December which was a festival especially important to slaves.

26. Letter about food (*Tab. Vindol.* II 302)

. . . .
f̣ạḅạe f̣renṣaẹ ṃ(odios) duos
pullos uiginti
malạ ṣị potes formonsa inueni-
re centum oua centum aut
ducenta si ibi · aequo emantur

. . . .

L.margin: ↓]rio mulsi si ẹḅr.[
]mus (sextarios) viii muriạẹ .[
].ṣ modium oliuae [
].ṇọ ⟦..ṃ⟧

Back: . . . .
traces
Verecundi
?traces

. . . bruised beans, two *modii*, chickens, twenty, a hundred apples, if you can find nice ones, a hundred or two hundred eggs, if they are for sale there at a fair price. . . . 8 *sextarii* of fish-sauce . . . a *modius* of olives . . . (Back) To . . . (?) slave of Verecundus.

Margin 2 The quantity of fish-sauce is probably preceded by a verb such as *misimus* ('we have sent').

Back 2 Since the addressee was a slave it is likely that the writer was also and that these are people responsible for domestic management in the *praetorium*.

27. Letter from Metto to Advectus (*Tab. Vindol.* II 309)

i

Meṭṭo Aduec̣to plurimam sụo
salutem
missi tibi materias per Saconem
modiola n(umero) xxxiiii
axses carrarios n(umero) xxxiix
inibi axsis tornaṭus n(umero) [i
radia n(umero) ccc
axses ad lectum n(umero) xxṿi
sessiones n(umero) viii
bruscas [n(umero)] ịị
pluṭeạ ṇ(umero) x̣x̣[

ii

]. n(umero) xxix
]..ilia n(umero) vi
] ṃissi tibi pelliculas caprinas n(umero) vi
uacat
m² [opto] bene ualeas frater

Back: *m*[1] *traces of 2 lines*

Metto(?) to his Advectus(?) very many greetings. I have sent you wooden materials through the agency of Saco:

hubs, number, 34
axles for carts, number, 38
therein an axle turned on the lathe, number, [1]
spokes, number, 300
planks (?) for a bed, number, 26
seats, number, 8 (?)
knots (?), number, 2 (?)
boards (?), number, 20+
. . ., number, 29
benches (?), number, 6
I have sent you goat-skins, number, 6

(2nd hand) I pray that (?) you are in good health, brother.

i.10 Knots of maple-wood were used in the manufacture of furniture according to Pliny, *Natural History*, 16.68.

ii.13 The suggested restoration is *sedilia*, although it is not clear precisely how these would differ from *sessiones*, mentioned in line 9.

28. Letter from Chrauttius to Veldeius (*Tab. Vindol.* II 310) PLATE VII

i

Chrauttius Veldeio suó fratri
contubernali antiquo plurimam salutem
et rogo te Veldei frater miror
quod ṃihi tot tempus nihil
rescripsti a parentibus nostris si quid audieris aut
Quoṭ.m in quo numero
sit et illum a me salutabis
⟦s⟧uerbis meis et Virilem
ueteriṇarium rogabis
illum ut forficem

ii

quam mihi promisṣịt pretio
mittas per aliquem de nosṭṛịṣ

et rogo te frater Virilis
salutẹs a me Ṭhuṭteṇam
sororem Velbuteịụm
rescribas nobis cụṃ..
se habeat *uacat*
*m*²? opto sis felicissimus
uale
Back:*m*¹ Londini
Veldedeio
equisioni co(n)s(ularis)
a Chrauttio
fṛạtre

Chrauttius to Veldeius, his brother and old messmate, very many greetings. And I ask you, brother Veldeius – I am surprised that you have written nothing back to me for such a long time – whether you have heard anything from our elders, or about . . . in which unit he is; and greet him from me in my words and Virilis the veterinary doctor. Ask him (sc. Virilis) whether you may send me through one of our friends the pair of shears which he promised me in exchange for money. And I ask you, brother Virilis, to greet from me our (?) sister Thuttena. Write back to us (?) how Velbuteius is (?). (2nd hand?) It is my wish that you enjoy the best of fortune. Farewell. (Back, 1st hand) (Deliver) at London. To Veldedeius, groom of the governor, from his brother Chrauttius.

1 A fragment of a letter to Flavius Cerialis (*Tab. Vindol.* II 264) may also be from Chrauttius. It is curious that the name of the addressee appears here as Veldeius and on the back as Veldedius; the first is perhaps a syncopated form.

18 The word we would expect at the end of the line is *quomodo* and it is uncertain whether the writer has simply made a mistake.

Back 1 Londini is a locative form and must indicate the place to which the letter was sent (cf. nos **29** and **30** and see *Tab. Vindol.* II, pp. 43–5). Presumably Veldeius disposed of it when he was at Vindolanda.

29. Letter from Sollemnis to Paris (*Tab. Vindol.* II 311)

i

Sollemnis Paridi fratri plurị-
mam salutẹ[m
ut scias me recte ualere

quod te inuicem fecisse
cupió · homo inpientissi-
me qui mihi ne unam e-
pistulam misisti sed
putó me humanius
facere qui tibi scribó

ii

. . . .
ṭibi f̣ṛaṭẹṛ [..]..[
contubernalem meum
salutabis a me Diligen-
tem et Cogitatum et
Corinthum et rogó
mittas mihi nómina
traces
. . . .

Margin: ↓]ṃ
]ṭer
]mẹ

Back: P̣aṛịḍị ...ḷuc̣.ọṛ.[
coh]ọrtis iii Batauo-
rum
a Sollemṇị
]....o

Sollemnis to Paris, his brother, very many greetings. I want you to know that I am in very good health, as I hope you are in turn, you neglectful man, who have sent me not even one letter. But I think that I am behaving in a more considerate fashion in writing to you . . . to you, brother, . . . my messmate. Greet from me Diligens and Cogitatus and Corinthus and I ask that you send me the names . . . Farewell, dearest brother (?). (Back) To Paris . . . of the 3rd Cohort of Batavians, from Sollemnis . . .

1 Although Greek names are not uncommon among the Batavians in the imperial guard, Paris is very unusual and unexpected. This, along with the names in ii.2–5, suggests the possibility that the people involved in this correspondence are slaves.

Back 1 It is very difficult to read the end of this line or to elucidate the connection between Paris and the 3rd Cohort of Batavians. He may be a slave of an officer or other member of that cohort.

30. Letter to Cessaucius Nigrinus (?) from Tullio (*Tab. Vindol.* II 312)

i

. . . .

traces

[*c.9*]ad quem cum p̣ṛịṃuṃ
[potes r]ọgo uenias habemus eniṃ
[*c.3*].[*c.4*].ạreṃ de rebus quas ṃiḥ[i
ṃịsseras non q. . . ille sciat
ẹ. . . . scṛị[p]sisseṣ.c̣. *traces*

ii

[*c.7* d]ẹḅeo tibi (denarios) x
[*c.6* Can]diduṃ et Nataḷem
[*c.5*]. .ụm rogo aliquiḍ
[*c.4*.]ọrum mihi miṭṭas
ṛ[ogo]Vir. .cium exc̣ịpịas beṇe

uacat

m^2? opto bene ualeaṣ uaḷ(e)
Back: m^1 Coris t. .st. *traces*
Cessaucio Ni.ṛịn[
dup(licario)
a Tullioni

. . . I ask you to come to him as soon as you are able. For we consider him a friend of ours (?). About the things which you had sent me . . . why he should know (?) . . . you (?) had written . . . I owe you 10 *denarii*. . . . Candidus and Natalis . . . I ask you to send me some . . . I ask you to give Viriocius (?) a warm welcome. (2nd hand?) I pray that you enjoy good health. Farewell. (Back, 1st hand) At Coria of the Textoverdi (?), to Cessaucius Nigrinus (?), *duplicarius*, from Tullio.

Back 1 The reading of the place name is not certain. Coria of the Textoverdi is a place mentioned in an inscription found at Vindolanda and therefore presumably in the region (*RIB* 1695, see *PNRB* 317–19).

31. Letter about the transport of stone (*Tab. Vindol.* II 316)

.[
quem modum carrulorum
missurus sis domine
deliberare tecum debes

ad lapidem portandum
Ṿoconti enim centụ[
carrulịs uno die la.[

L.margin: ↓ . . . .

m[2] nisi rogas Vocontị[
ut lepidem exp̣[
non explicabi[
rogo ụṭ rescri[bas
quid uelis me [
opto benẹ [ualeas

. . . you ought to decide, my lord, what quantity of wagons you are going to send to carry stone. For the century of Vocontius . . . on one day with wagons . . . Unless you ask Vocontius to sort out (?) the stone, he will not sort it out. I ask you to write what you want me to do (?). I pray that you are in good health.

Margin 2 *lepidem* appears to be a mistake for *lapidem*.

32. Letter from Octavius to Candidus (*Tab. Vindol.* II 343) PLATE VIII

i

Octauius Candido fratri suo
salutem
a Marino nerụi pondo centum
explicabo e quo tu de hac
re scripseras ne mentiọnem
mihi fecit aliquotiens tibi
scripseram sp̣icas me emisse
prọp̣e m(odios) quinque milia prop-
ter quod (denarii) mihi necessari sunt
nisi mittis mi aliquit (denariorum)

ii

minime quingentos futurum
est ut quod arre dedi perdam
(denarios) circa trecentos et erubes-
cam ita rogo quam primum aliquit
(denariorum) mi mitte coria que scribis
esse Cataractonio scribe
dentur mi et karrum de quo

scribis et quit sit cum eo ḳarro
mi scribe iam illec peṭissem
nissi iumenṭa non curaui uexsaṛe
dum uiae male sunt uịde cum Tertio
de (denariis) viii s(emisse) quos a Fatale accepit
non illos mi *uacat* accepto tulit

iii

sciṭọ ṃae explesse [[exple]] coria
clxx et bracis excussi habeo
m(odios) cxịx fac (denarios) mi mittas ut possi-
ṃ spicam habere in excusso-
rio iam autem si quit habui
perexcussi contuber-
nalis Fronti amici hic fuerat
desiderabat coria ei ad-
signarem et ita (denarios) datur-
{ur}us erat dixi ei coria in-
tra K(alendas) Martias daturum Idibus

iv

Ianuariis constituerat se uentur-
um nec interuenit̩ nec curauit
accipere cum haberẹt coriạ si
pecuniam ḍaret dabam ei Fronti-
nium Iulium audio magno lice-
re pro coriaṭione quem hic
comparauit (denarios) quinos
saluta Spectatum I . . . -
ṛiuṃ Firmum
epistulas a Gleụçone accepi
uạḷ(e)

Back: Vindol

Octavius to his brother Candidus, greetings. The hundred pounds of sinew from Marinus – I will settle up. From the time when you wrote about this matter, he has not even mentioned it to me. I have several times written to you that I have bought about five thousand *modii* of ears of grain, on account of which I need cash. Unless you send me some cash, at least five hundred *denarii*, the result will be that I shall lose what I have laid out as a deposit,

about three hundred *denarii*, and I shall be embarrassed. So, I ask you, send me some cash as soon as possible. The hides which you write are at Cataractonium – write that they be given to me and the wagon about which you write. And write to me what is with that wagon. I would have already been to collect them except that I did not care to injure the animals while the roads are bad. See with Tertius about the 8 1/2 *denarii* which he received from Fatalis. He has not credited them to my account. Know that I have completed the 170 hides and I have 119 (?) *modii* of threshed *bracis*. Make sure that you send me some cash so that I may have ears of grain on the threshing-floor. Moreover, I have already finished threshing all that I had. A messmate of our friend Frontius has been here. He was wanting me to allocate (?) him hides and that being so, was ready to give cash. I told him I would give him the hides by the Kalends of March. He decided that he would come on the Ides of January. He did not turn up nor did he take any trouble to obtain them since he had hides. If he had given the cash, I would have given him them. I hear that Frontinius Julius has for sale at a high price the leather ware (?) which he bought here for five *denarii* apiece. Greet Spectatus and . . . and Firmus. I have received letters from Gleuco. Farewell.
(Back) (Deliver) at Vindolanda.

ii.16 Cataractonium (Catterick) is known to have been an important centre of tanning and leather-production at this period, see Burnham and Wacher (1990), 111–17.

iii.26–7 The word division *possi/m* is bizarre and unexpected.

iv.42–3 The second name is very difficult to read. The common name *Ianuarium* is a possibility (see A. R. Birley (1991), 91).

Back It is curious that the place to which the letter was to be taken is mentioned (see above, **27**.back 1 note) but the name of the recipient is not written. Presumably the letter was delivered by someone who knew Candidus.

33. Appeal or petition (*Tab. Vindol.* II 344)

i

eo ṃagis me ca[*c.12*]
d...[ ]em mercem [*c.8*]
r[..] uel effunder[*c.3*]ṛ[
[..]mine probo tuam maies-
[t]atem imploro ne patiaris me
[i]nnocentem uirgis caṣ[t]ịgatum
esse et domine proụ[.]. prae-

[fe]c̣ṭo non potui queri quia ua-
[let]udini detinebatur
queṣ[tu]s sum beneficiario

ii

[*c.8* ce]nturionibu[s
[*c.7*] ṇụmeri eius .[
[*c.3* tu]ạm misericord[ia]m
impḷoro ne patiaris me
hominem trasmarinum
et innocentem de cuius f[ide
inquiras uirgis cruenṭ[at]u[m
esse ac si aliquid sceler[i]ṣ
commisissem *uacat*

. . . he beat (?) me all the more . . . goods . . . or pour them down the drain (?). As befits an honest man (?) I implore your majesty not to allow me, an innocent man, to have been beaten with rods and, my lord, inasmuch as (?) I was unable to complain to the prefect because he was detained by ill-health I have complained in vain (?) to the *beneficiarius* and the rest (?) of the centurions of (?) his unit. I accordingly implore your mercifulness not to allow me, a man from overseas and an innocent one, about whose good faith you may inquire, to have been bloodied by rods as if I had committed some crime.

i. 1–4 The restoration suggested (*exempli gratia*) is *eo ṃagis me ca[stigauit dum] / ḍịc̣ẹ[r]em mercem [nihil uale-]/r[e] / uel effunder[em. p] ṛ[o] / [ho]mine probo* etc.

i. 10 for the *beneficiarius* see **6**.18 note.

ii. 11–12 The restoration suggested is *queṣ[tu]s sum beneficiario / frustra et ce]ṇturionibụ[s / ceteris] ṇụmeri eius* etc. This is based on the idea that the appellant was complaining about having been beaten by a centurion.

34. Letter about clothing (*Tab. Vindol.* II 346)

i

. . . .

traces

ṛạm tibi paria udoṇ[um
ṭ. ab Sattua solearuṃ [
duo · et subligarioruṃ [
duo solearum paria dụ[o

traces

. . . .

ii

. . . .

]um ṣaluṭa. . . [
]ṇdem Elpidem Ịụ[
]. enum Tetrịcum et omṇ[es
[c]ontibernales cum quibus
[o]p̣to felicissimus uiuas *uacat*[

. . . .

. . . I have sent (?) you . . . pairs of socks from Sattua two pairs of sandals and two pairs of underpants, two pairs of sandals . . . Greet . . . ndes, Elpis, Iu . . ., . . . enus, Tetricus and all your messmates with whom I pray that you live in the greatest good fortune.

3 It is possible that the letters at the beginning of the line are *ti*, suggesting the end of *uiginti* ('twenty'). Since what precedes is incomplete it is unclear whether *ab Sattua* should be taken with the socks or with the sandals and underpants in the following phrase; the latter is more likely in view of the repetition of sandals in line 5.

Corrigenda Since the first publication of this book, some corrections and improvements to the foregoing texts have been made or suggested:

No. 1, line 12: the last word before the numeral is probably *Gallia*, suggesting that this group was absent in Gaul.
Line 14: perhaps read *Eb]uraco stipendiatum* ('At York, to fetch pay'). [Tomlin (1996), 461]

No. 4, line 4: the formula should be understood not as *q(ui) uidebunt*, but as *qui debunt* ('all are at their posts who ought to be'). [See Adams (1995), 102–3 and cf. the form *habunt* in no. 37, line 14, below]

No. 7, line 3: *lignis* should be translated as 'firewood'. [Tomlin (1996), 461]

No. 20, lines 11–14: Tomlin (1996), 463 suggests the following reading and translation: *scis certe hoc me u[er-]/sute impetrare cum sim [an-]/nonarius et iam adep[tus] / translationem*, 'you well know that I am smart in getting hold of this, since I am the commissariat officer and have acquired transport'.

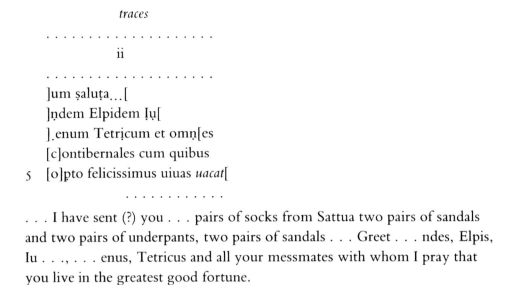

No.25, line 3: J.N. Adams has shown that the word *souxtum* is a celticised misspelling of the Latin word *sumptum* ('expenditure'). [Adams (1995), 93–4]

Additional texts

The following texts were discovered in the excavations of 1991–4. For the full editions see Bowman and Thomas (1996) and Birley and Birley (1994).

35. Account of clothing, equestrian equipment, utensils and textiles (Bowman and Thomas 1996, no.1)

i

1]....suras n(umero) ii ·s(ingularis)· (denarios) iii s(emissem) .[
2 f(iunt) (denarii) v[ii
3 infiblatoria n(umero) vi ·s(ingulare)· (denarios) xi ṣ(emissem)
4 f(iunt) (denarii) lxix
5 capitularia n(umero) v ·s(ingulare)· (denarii) s(emissem) (quadrantem)
6 f(iunt) (denarii) iii s(emis) (q̣ụạḍṛạṇṣ)
7 capillamenti p̣(ondo) viiii
8 lib(ras) ·s(ingularem)· (denarios) v s(emissem) (q̣ụạḍṛạṇṭẹṃ) f(iunt) (denarii) li s(emis) (quadrans)
9 lumbaria n(umero) x ·s(ingulare)· (denarios) ii s(emissem) f(iunt) (denarii) xxv
10 scordiscum n(umero) i *uacat* (denarios) ⟦v⟧xii
11 ⟦saga corticia n(umero) xṿ ṣ⟧

ii

12 sa]ga corticia n(umero) xṿ m[
13] in ·m( )· s(ingularem)· (denarios) iii f(iunt) (denarii) ccxxx̣v[
14 sarcinas n(umero) x ·s(ingularem)· (denarios) s(emissem) (octantem) (assem i) f(iunt) (denarii) vi ṣ(emis) [(quadrans) (octans)
15 trullas n(umero) ⟦v⟧iiii ·s(ingularem)· (denarios) v (assem i) f(iunt) (denarii) xx (q̣ụạḍṛạṇṣ)
16 trullas n(umero) iiii ·s(ingularem)· (denarios) iii s(emissem) (quadrantem) (octantem) (assem i) f(iunt) (denarii) xv s(emis) (quadrans)

17 trullas n(umero) iiii ·s(ingularem)· (denarios) ii s(emissem) (quadrantem) (octantem) (assem i) f(iunt) (denarii) xi ṣ(emis) [(quadrans)

18 frẹnos n(umero) ii ·s(ingularem)· (denarios) iii s(emissem) f(iunt) (denarii) vịị

19 uelum coccini(um) ·i· m( ) xi s(emis) f(iunt) (denarii) liiii s(emis) .

20 uelum uirdem ·i· m( ) xi s(emis) f(iunt) (denarii) xlvi s(emis) .

21 uela purp(urea) ·ii· m( ) xị s(emis) f(iunt) (denarii) lxxxịịx s(emis) (q̣ụạḍṛạṇṣ)

22 uelum ...... ·i· m( ) x s(emis) f(iunt) (denarii) lv .

Necklace-locks (?), number 2, 3½+ *denarii* each, total 7+ *denarii.*
Cloaks, number 6, 11½ *denarii* each, total 69 *denarii.*
Headbands, number 5, ¾ *denarius* each, total 3¾ *denarii.*
Hair, 9 pounds in weight, 5¾ *denarii* per pound, total 51¾ *denarii.*
Drawers, number 10, 2½ *denarii* each, total 25 *denarii.*
Saddle (?), number 1, 12 *denarii.*
Cloaks made of bark (?), number 15 (?), ...
Cloaks made of bark (?), number 15, measure(s) (?) .., 3 *denarii* per measure (?), total 235+ *denarii.*
Bags, number 10, ⅝ *denarius* and 1 *as* each, total 6⅞ *denarii.*
Skillets, number 4, 5 *denarii* 1 *as* each, total 20¼ *denarii.*
Skillets, number 4, 3⅞ *denarii* and 1 *as* each, total 15¾ *denarii.*
Skillets, number 4, 2⅞ *denarii* and 1 *as* each, total 11¾ *denarii.*
Reins, number 2, 3½ *denarii* each, total 7 *denarii.*
Scarlet curtain (?), 1, measuring 11½, total 54½+ *denarii.*
Green curtain (?), 1, measuring 11½, total 46½+ *denarii.*
Purple curtains (?), 2, measuring 11 1/2, total 88¾ (?) *denarii.*
... curtain (?), 1, measuring 10½, total 55+ *denarii.*

i.1 The traces of the first word are compatible with *clausuras.*

ii.13, 19–22 The abbreviation *m( ),* written with a medial dot before and after it in line 13 and with a superscript dash in lines 19–22, elsewhere stands for *modius,* a dry or liquid measure, which the context rules out here. It is possible that it should be understood here as *modus, modulus,* or *mensura,* signifying a unit of measurement for textiles.

36. Account of poultry, AD 102–4 (Bowman and Thomas 1996, no.2, abr.)

Five or six half-leaves from a notebook containing domestic accounts of the *praetorium* in the period when it was occupied by Flavius Cerialis and his family.

Front: A	*traces* [ ] ab .[
2	ịii Idus Aprịl[es
3	decurioṇ[
4	·i· c̣eru[
5	xvii K(alendas) Iunia[s
6	ceruesaṛ[io
7	xv K(alendas) Iunias a[
8	pulli .[
9	Traiano v[
10	vi K(alendas) Maias .[
11	ab Crescenṭ[e
	uacat
12	eodem die ạḅ .[
13	anseṛẹṣ [
B	Nonis Iun[is
15	suetio adiụ[
16	iiii Idus Iunias [
17	ceruesario [
18	iii Idus Iunias [
19	Vattone ...[
20	{K I}Sex(to) Attio
	Subuṛ[ano
21	K(alendis) Ianuarịs ab .[
22	ueterạno p̣uḷ[l-
23	eodem die ạb Saụ.[
24	ab Chnisson[e
25	iiii Nonas Ianuarịạ[s
26	pulli [ ].[
C	K(alendis) Martis ab Mạ..[
28	eodem die ab C̣an[

29	iii K(alendas) Apriles ab
	Mar[
30	pr(idie) K(alendas) Apriles
	ab Exṣ[
31	⟦·ḳ ....s⟧ *uacat*
32	viiii K(alendas) Maias ab
	Ṿ[
33	iumenṭaṛio ḅṛ..[
34	summa anṣ[er-
35	item anserẹ[s
36	pulli ạdempṭ[i
37	item adempti [
38	pulli [
39	pr(idie) K(alendas) Maias
	uacat?
40	item pulli a[
41	per c̣omm[
42	summa pul[l-
D	ịiii Ḳ(alendas) ......[
44	].sẹ[
45	expensa[
46	xv K(alendas) Iunias m[
47	nas pullus [
48	eodem die cena.[
49	aḅsumptus p̣[ullus
50	ṿiii K(alendas) Iunias [
51	nio pullụṣ [
52	Idibus Iunis c̣[
53	legati [
54	xviii K(alendas) Iuḷịaṣ [
55	C̣oriṣ iussụ [

56	⟦ *traces* ṣ⟧
57	eodem die ịṇ . [
58	perierunṭ [
uacat	
E	
Blank	
Back:	
E back	ịịii Idus Iunias [
60	missiọ Flaui[
61	iii K(alendas) Septembres
	.[
62	Nigro Broccho [
63	viii K(alendas) ⟦Ṃaịas⟧
	Ian[uarias
64	ceṇantẹ Brocch[o
65	K(alendis) Ianuaris p̣er[
66	...[
67	xvi K(alendas) Febrụ[arias
68	Brocch[o
69	viiii K(alendas) Mar̩[t]ịa[s
70	a stabụlo [
71	K(alendis) Martis ḍoṃ[
72	matronar̩[
D back	Idibus Martịs .[
74	Nigro et ..e.[
75	xii K(alendas) Apriles ab[
76	ṇae [
77	pr(idie) Nonas Ap̣ṛiḷeṣ [
78	Broccho [
79	iii K(alendas) Maias pr..[
80	Septembrẹ ..[
81	ịiiị Nonas Maịạṣ [
82	apud Sautenụṃ [
83	summa expeṇ[sorum
84	reliqụ..[
85	et anseres ṇ(umero) [
86	ex.[ ].[
C back	ṿii Idus Maias [
88	Onesimo aḍ si.[
89	eodem die Sauteṇ[o
90	in stabuló . [
91	iiii K(alendas) Iunias
	prandeṇ[
92	et Flauino ab[
93	eodem die mor̩[
94	apud Sauteṇ[um
95	K(alendis) Maiarum sịṃ[
96	aduentu consụ[laris
97	ịṇ prandịọ abṣụ[mpt-
98	item Ç̣orịs m....[
99	ṿiii Idus Iunias .[
100	pulli n(umero) ịịịị[

A

. . . from . . .
11 (?) April
(from?) the decurion(s)
of the 1st . . .beer (?) . . .
16 May, (from?) . . .
the brewer . . .
18 May, from (?) . . .
chickens . . .
In the 5th consulship of Trajan
27 April . . .
from Crescens . . .
on the same day, from . . .
geese . . .

B

5 June, (from?) . . .
Suetius (?) . . .

10 June, (from?) . . .
the brewer . . .
11 June, (from?) . . .
Vatto . . .
In the consulship of Sex. Attius Suburanus
1 January, from . . .
veteran, chickens . . .
on the same day, from Sautenus (?) . . .
from Chnisso . . .
2 January . . .
chickens . . .

18 May . . .
. . . a chicken
on the same day, at dinner (?) . . .
a chicken (?) consumed
25 May . . .
. . ., a chicken . . .
13 June . . .
the legate . . .
14 June
at Coria, on the instructions of . . .
on the same day in . . .
there have died . . .

C

1 March, from Ma. . .
on the same day, from Candidus (?)
30 March, from Mar. . .
31 March, from Exspeditus (?) . . .
23 April, from V. . .
in charge of the draft-animals . . .
total, geese. . .
likewise, geese . . .
nursling chicks (?) . . .
likewise, nurslings (?) . . .
chickens . . .
30 April
likewise, chickens . . .
through Commodus (?) . . .
total, chickens . . .

D

29 May (?)
. . .
expended . . .

E back

10 June . . .
discharge of Flavinus (?) . . .
30 August . . .
Niger and Brocchus . . .
25 December
when Brocchus was dining
1 January, through (?) . . .
. . . .
17 January . . .
Brocchus . . .
21 February . . .
from the pen . . .
1 March, for the lord(s) (?) . . .
on the Matronalia (?) . . .

D back

15 March . . .
Niger and . . .
21 March, . . .
. . .

4 April . . .
Brocchus . . .
29 April, . . .
September . . .
4 May . . .
with Sautenus . . .
total expended . . .
remainder . . .
and geese, number . . .
. . .

C back 9 May . . .
for (?) Onesimus with the standards (?) . . .
on the same day, for
Sautenus (?) . . .
in the pen . . .
29 May as lunch for . . .
and Flavinus, consumed (?) . . .
on the same day, . . .
with Sautenus . . .
1 May . . .
at the visit of the governor
. . .
consumed at lunch . . .
likewise at Coria . . .
6 June . . .
chickens, number 4 (?)
. . .

A.9 A reference to the fifth consulship of the emperor Trajan, AD 103.

B.20 The consular date is AD 104.

E back.63 The erasure of *Maias* and the substitution of *Ianuarias* shows clearly that this is not a running 'day-book' compiled as and when the commodities were received, used or paid for, but an account compiled retrospectively.

C back.96 For another possible reference to a visit of the provincial governor to Vindolanda see no.18.9–11.

37. Letter from Masclus to Flavius Cerialis (Bowman and Thomas 1996, no.3)

i

Masclus Ceriali regi suọ
salutem
cras quid uelis nos fecissẹ
rogó dómine pṛạẹ-
c̣ịp̣iás utrum[n]ẹ
cum uexsilló · omnes
rediemus an alter-
ni c̣....ṛum · aeque

ii

Two lines missing
felicisṣiṃ[u]ṣ [
et sis mihi propitius
Space of one line
ceruesam commilitones
non habunt quam
rogó iubeas mitti

Back:
F̣[l]ạụịo C̣ẹṛịạḷi
p̣raef(ecto)
Space of one line
a Masclo dec(urione)

Masclus to Cerialis his king, greeting. Please, my lord, give instructions (?) as to what you want us to have done tomorrow. Are we all to return with the standard or only half of us? . . . most fortunate and be well-disposed towards me. My fellow-soldiers have no beer. Please order some to be sent. (Back) To Flavius Cerialis, prefect, from Masclus, decurion.

i.1 *Tab. Vindol.* II 505 is a fragmentary letter from a decurion named Masculus, certainly the same man. The syncope in the spelling of the name is not unexpected, see Adams (1995), 92. The title *rex* is not found elsewhere in the tablets, but, despite the fact that the Batavian units are known to have been commanded by nobles of royal blood (Tacitus, *Histories* 4.12–13), it is more likely that it here simply means 'patron', a well-attested usage.

ii.14 For the form *habunt* instead of *habent*, see above, Corrigenda (No.4, line 4).

38. Business letter from Maior to Maritimus (Birley and Birley 1994, no. 4, Bowman and Thomas 1996, Appendix)

i

Maior Maritim[o] ṣ[uo
salutem
scire te uọlui epistulas mihi mis-
sas esse ab patri meó in qui-

bus scribit mihi ut ei no-
tum faciam quid gesseró de
fussá quod sị itá gessịsti
negotium cum cạesạrịa-
ṇis fac ut certum mịhi
[r]ẹ[s]ṣc̣ṛibas ut egó pạ[tri

ii

meo sic resscribere
possim si quid inter-
numeraueris egọ ṭibi
sine morá brạc̣em ex-
pellam pro s⟦.⟧ummá
quod effịciatur egó
cum hạec tibị scribẹ-
rem lectum calfacieba[m
opto sis felicissimu[s
salutat te p̣ạ[ter m]ẹ[us
uaḷ[e
Left margin:
[rogo s]ị puerum missurus es mịttes chiṛ[o-
[grafum] cum eo quo securior sim

Back:
Vindolaṇde
Coccẹḷió Mari-
timó
[a Ma]ị[o]ṛe

Maior to his Maritimus greeting. I wanted you to know that a letter has been sent to me by my father in which he writes to me that I should make known to him what I have done about the spindle(?). As to which, if you have had business in that regard with the *Caesariani* see that you write back to me with clear information so that I can similarly write back to my father. If you have made any payment as an intermediary(?), I will issue(?) corn to you without delay in proportion to the sum [which you have spent]. Let this be done.

When I was writing this to you I was making the bed warm. I wish you may be in the best of fortune. My father sends you his greetings. Farewell.
(Left margin) If you intend to send a boy please send a note of hand with him so that I may be the more reassured.
(Back) [Deliver] at Vindolanda. To Coccelius(?) Maritimus from Maior.

i.7 The word *fussa*, if correctly read, might refer to a spindle as a component of a grain-mill.

i.8–9 The term *caesariani* here probably refers to imperial freedmen.

Back.25 The reading of the name as *Coccelio* is not certain; *Cocceiio* (for *Cocceio*) is also possible.

BIBLIOGRAPHY

J. N. Adams (1977), *The Vulgar Latin of the letters of Claudius Terentianus.* Manchester

J. N. Adams (1995), 'The Language of the Vindolanda writing tablets: an interim report', *JRS* 85: 86–134

L. Allason-Jones (1989), *Women in Roman Britain.* London

J. Andre (1981), *L'alimentation et la cuisine à Rome.* Paris

A. R. Birley (1979), *The people of Roman Britain.* London

A. R. Birley (1981), *The Fasti of Roman Britain.* Oxford

A. R. Birley (1990a), 'Vindolanda; new writing-tablets 1986–9', in Maxfield and Dobson (ed. 1990): 16–20

A. R. Birley (1990b), *Officers of the Second Augustan Legion in Britain.* Cardiff

A. R. Birley (1991), 'Vindolanda: notes on some new writing tablets', *ZPE* 88: 87–102

E. Birley (1988), *The Roman army, Papers 1929–86.* Amsterdam

R. E. Birley (1977), *Vindolanda. A Roman frontier post on Hadrian's Wall.* London

R. E. Birley (1990), *The Roman documents from Vindolanda.* Newcastle upon Tyne

A. R. Birley, R. E. Birley (1994), 'Four new writing-tablets from Vindolanda', *ZPE* 100: 431–46

B. Bischoff (1990), *Latin palaeography, antiquity and the middle ages.* Cambridge

M. C. Bishop (ed. 1985), *The production and distribution of Roman military equipment.* British Archaeological Reports, Int. Ser. 275

M. C. Bishop (1985), 'The military fabrica and the production of arms in the early principate', in Bishop (ed. 1985): 1–42

M. C. Bishop, J. C. N. Coulston (1993), *Roman military equipment.* London

M. C. Bishop, J. N. Dore (1988), *Corbridge, excavation of the Roman fort and town 1947–80.* London

T. F. C. Blagg, A. C. King (ed. 1984), *Military and civilian in Roman Britain: cultural relationships in a frontier province.* British Archaeological Reports, Brit. Ser. 136

T. F. C. Blagg, M. Millett (ed. 1990), *The early Roman empire in the west.* Oxford

J. H. F. Bloemers (1983), 'Acculturation in the Rhine/Meuse Basin in the Roman period: a preliminary survey', in Brandt and Slofstra (ed. 1983): 159–210

A. K. Bowman (1975), 'The Vindolanda writing-tablets and the development of the Roman book form', *ZPE* 18: 237–52

A. K. Bowman (1991), 'Literacy in the Roman empire: mass and mode', in Humphrey (ed. 1991): 119–31

A. K. Bowman (1994), 'The Roman imperial army: letters and literacy on the northern frontier', in Bowman and Woolf (ed. 1994), 109–25

A. K. Bowman, J. D. Thomas (1987), 'New texts from Vindolanda', *Britannia* 18: 125–42

A. K. Bowman, J. D. Thomas, J. N. Adams (1990), 'Two letters from Vindolanda', *Britannia* 21: 33–52

A. K. Bowman, J. D. Thomas (1991), 'A military strength report from Vindolanda', *JRS* 81: 62–73

A. K. Bowman, J. D. Thomas (1996), 'New writing-tablets from Vindolanda', *Britannia* 27: 299–328

A. K. Bowman, G. D. Woolf (1994), *Literacy and power in the ancient World*. Cambridge

R. Brandt, J. Slofstra (ed. 1983), *Roman and native in the Low Countries*. British Archaeological Reports, Int. Ser. 184

D. J. Breeze (1974), 'The organisation of the career structure of the immunes and principales of the Roman army', *Bonner Jahrbücher* 174: 245–92

D. J. Breeze (1984), 'Demand and supply on the northern frontier', in Miket and Burgess (ed. 1984): 32–68

D. J. Breeze, B. Dobson (1985), 'Roman military deployment in north England', *Britannia* 16: 1–19

B. C. Burnham, H. B. Johnson (ed. 1979), *Invasion and response: the case of Roman Britain*. British Archaeological Reports, Brit. Ser.73

B. C. Burnham, J. S. Wacher (1990), *The 'small towns' of Roman Britain*. London

J. Collingwood Bruce (1975), *Lapidarium septentrionale*. Newcastle upon Tyne

J. Collingwood Bruce (1978), *Handbook to the Roman Wall*. 13th edn by C. M. Daniels, Newcastle upon Tyne

R. M. Butler (ed. 1971), *Soldier and civilian in Roman Yorkshire*. Leicester

P. J. Casey (1982), 'Civilians and soldiers – friends, Romans, countrymen?' in Clack and Haselgrove (ed. 1982): 123–32

P. A. G. Clack, 'The northern frontier: farmers in the military zone', in Miles (ed. 1982): 377–402

P. A. G. Clack, S. Haselgrove (ed. 1982), *Rural settlement in the Roman north*. Durham

P. Cugusi (1983), *Evoluzione e forme dell'epistolografia latina nella tarda repubblica e nei primi due secoli dell'impero*. Rome

P. Cugusi (1987), 'Leggendo le tavolette latine di Vindolanda', *Rivista di filologia e di istruzione classica* 115: 113–21.

B. Cunliffe (ed. 1988), *The temple of Sulis Minerva at Bath*, Volume 2, *The finds from the sacred spring*. Oxford University Committee for Archaeology, Monograph 16

C. Daniels (1989), 'The Flavian and Trajanic northern frontier', in Todd (ed. 1989): 31–5

G. B. Dannell, J.-P. Wild (1987), *Longthorpe II: the military works depot*. Britannia Monograph 8. London

S. Daris (1964), *Documenti per la storia dell'esercito romano in Egitto*. Milan

R. W. Davies (1974), 'The daily life of the Roman soldier under the principate,' *ANRW* II.1: 299–338.

R. W. Davies (1989), *Service in the Roman Army*. Ed. D. J. Breeze, V. A. Maxfield, Edinburgh

C. Dickson (1989), 'The Roman diet in Britain and Germany', *Archäobotanik. Dissertationes Botanicae* 133: 135–54

K. R. Dixon, P. Southern (1992), *The Roman cavalry*. London

B. Dobson, J. C. Mann (1973), 'The Roman army in Britain and Britons in the Roman army', *Britannia* 4: 191–205

C. van Driel-Murray (1985), 'The production and supply of military leatherwork in the first and second centuries A.D.: a review of the archaeological evidence', in Bishop (ed. 1985): 43–81

R. P. Duncan-Jones (1982), *The economy of the Roman empire, quantitative studies*. 2nd edn, Cambridge

D. Ellis Evans (1983), 'Language contact in pre-Roman and Roman Britain', *ANRW* II.29.2: 949–87

S. S. Frere (1987), *Britannia, a history of Roman Britain*. 3rd edn, London

S. S. Frere, J. J. Wilkes (1989), *Strageath, excavations within the Roman fort 1973–86*. Britannia Monograph 9. London

M. Fulford (1984), 'Demonstrating Britannia's economic dependence in the first and second centuries', in Blagg and King (ed. 1984): 129–42

M. Fulford (1991), Britain and the Roman empire: the evidence for regional and long distance trade', in R. F. J. Jones (1991): 45–8

D. Ganz (1990), 'On the history of Tironian notes', in P. F. Ganz (ed. 1990): 35–51

P. F. Ganz (ed. 1990), *Tironische Noten*. Wiesbaden

W. Glasbergen, W. Groenman-van Waateringe 1974 *The Pre-Flavian garrisons of Valkenburg Z. H.* Amsterdam

W. S. Hanson (1987), *Agricola and the conquest of the north*. London

B. R. Hartley, J. S. Wacher (ed. 1983), *Roman and her northern provinces*. Gloucester

M. Hassall (1970), 'Batavians and the Roman conquest of Britain', *Britannia* 1: 131–6

M. Hassall (1973), 'Roman soldiers in Roman London', in Strong (ed. 1973): 231–7

M. Hassall (1978), 'Britain and the Rhine provinces: epigraphic evidence for Roman trade', in Taylor and Cleere (ed. 1978): 41–8

M. Hassall (1983), 'The internal planning of Roman auxiliary forts', in Hartley and Wacher (ed. 1983): 96–131

D. Haupt, H. G. Horn (ed. 1977), *Studien zur den Militärgrenzen Roms: Vorträge des 10. internationalen Limeskongresses in der Germania Inferior. Bonner Jahrbücher* Beih. 38

N. J. Higham (1991), 'Soldiers and settlement in northern England', in R. F. J. Jones (ed. 1991): 93–102

L. Hird (1977), *Vindolanda V: the pre-Hadrianic pottery*. Hexham

G. W. I. Hodgson (1976), *The animals of Vindolanda*. Newcastle upon Tyne

G. W. I. Hodgson (1977), *Vindolanda II: the animal remains*. Hexham

P. A. Holder (1980), *Studies in the auxilia of the Roman army from Augustus to Trajan*. British Archaeological Reports, Int. Ser. 80

P. A. Holder (1982), *The Roman Army in Britain*. London

C. J. Howgego (1992), 'The supply and use of money in the Roman world 200 B.C. – A.D. 300', *JRS* 82: 1–31

J. H. Humphrey (ed. 1991), *Literacy in the*

Roman world. Journal of Roman Archaeology, Suppl. 4

B. ISAAC (1992), *The limits of empire, the Roman army in the east.* 2nd edn, Oxford

G. D. B. JONES (1984), '"Becoming different without knowing it". The role and development of *vici*', in Blagg and King (ed. 1984): 75–91

G. D. B. JONES, D. J. MATTINGLY (1990), *An atlas of Roman Britain.* Oxford

G. D. B. JONES (1990), 'The emergence of the Tyne-Solway frontier', in Maxfield and Dobson (ed. 1990): 98–107

M. JONES (1991), 'Food production and consumption – plants', in R. J. F. Jones (ed. 1991): 21–8

R. J. F. JONES (ed. 1991), *Britain in the Roman period: recent trends.* Sheffield

A. C. KING (1984), 'Animal bones and the dietary identity of military and civilian groups in Roman Britain, Germany and Gaul', in Blagg and King (ed. 1984): 187–218

A. C. KING (1991), 'Food production and consumption – meat', in R. F. J. Jones (ed. 1991): 15–20

J. KRAMER (1991) 'Die Verwendung des Apex und P. Vindob. L I c', *ZPE* 88: 141–50

E. LALOU (ed. 1992), *Les tablettes à écrire de l'antiquité à l'époque moderne. Bibliologia* 12. Brepols-Turnhout

R. MARICHAL, 'Les tablettes à écrire dans le monde romain', in Lalou (ed. 1992): 165–85

V. A. MAXFIELD (1986), 'Pre-Flavian forts and their garrisons', *Britannia* 17: 59–72

V. A. MAXFIELD, M. J. DOBSON (ed. 1990), *Roman frontier studies 1989, Proceedings of the XVth International Congress of Roman Frontier Studies.* Exeter

R. MCKITTERICK (ed. 1990), *The uses of literacy in early medieval Europe.* Cambridge

P. S. MIDDLETON (1979), 'Army supply in Roman Gaul: an hypothesis for Roman Britain', in Burnham and Johnson (ed. 1979): 81–97

R. MIKET, C. BURGESS (ed. 1984), *Between and beyond the Walls. Essays on the pre-history and history of north Britain in honour of George Jobey.* Edinburgh

D. MILES (ed. 1982), *The Romano-British countryside.* British Archaeological Reports, Brit. Ser. 103

M. MILLETT (1990), *The Romanization of Britain.* Cambridge

N. P. MILNER (1993), *Vegetius: Epitome of military science.* Liverpool

A. MÓCSY (1983), 'The Civilized Pannonians of Velleius', in Hartley and Wacher (ed. 1983): 169–78

A. OLIVER, J. SHELTON (1979), 'Silver on papyrus', *Archaeology* 32: 22–8

B. RAWSON (ed. 1986), *The family in ancient Rome, new perspectives.* London

I. A. RICHMOND (1953), 'Three Roman writing-tablets from London', *Antiquaries Journal* 33: 206–8.

M. M. ROXAN (1991), 'Women on the frontiers', in Maxfield and Dobson (ed. 1990): 462–7

N. ROYMANS (1990), *Tribal societies in Northern Gaul, an anthropological perspective.* Amsterdam

J. SMEESTERS, 'Les Tungri dans l'armée romaine, état actuel des nos connaissances', in Haupt and Horn (ed. 1977): 175–86

M. A. Speidel (1992), 'Roman army pay scales', *JRS* 82: 87–106
M. P. Speidel (1978), *Guards of the Roman Armies*. Antiquitas, Reihe 1.28. Bonn
M. P. Speidel (1984), *Roman Army Studies* I. Amsterdam
M. P. Speidel (1985), 'Furlough in the Roman Army', *Yale Classical Studies* 28: 283–93.
M. P. Speidel (1989), 'The soldiers' servants', *Ancient Society* 20: 239–47
J. Stevenson (1990), 'Literacy in Ireland: the evidence of the Patrick dossier in the Book of Armagh', in McKitterick (ed. 1990): 11–35
K. Strobel (1987), 'Anmerkungen zur Geschichte der Bataverkohorten in der hohen Kaiserzeit', *ZPE* 70: 271–92
D. E. Strong (1966), *Greek and Roman gold and silver plate*. London
D. E. Strong (ed. 1973), *Archaeological theory and practice*. London
J. du Plat Taylor, H. Cleere (ed. 1978), *Roman shipping and trade: Britain and the Rhine provinces*. Council for British Archaeology, Research Report 24. London
J. C. Teitler (1985), *Notarii and exceptores*. Amsterdam
J. D. Thomas (1992), 'The Latin writing-tablets from Vindolanda in north Britain', in Lalou (ed. 1992): 203–9
J. D. Thomas, R. W. Davies (1977), 'A new military strength report on papyrus', *JRS* 67: 50–61
J.-O. Tjäder (1986), review of *Tab. Vindol.* I, *Scriptorium* 50: 297–301
M. Todd (ed. 1989), *Research on Roman Britain 1960–89*. Britannia Monograph 11. London
R. S. O. Tomlin (1986), 'Roman Britain in 1985', *Britannia* 17: 450–2
R. S. O. Tomlin (1988), 'The curse tablets', in Cunliffe (ed. 1988): 4–277
R. S. O. Tomlin (1992), 'The Twentieth Legion at Wroxeter and Carlisle in the first century: the epigraphic evidence', *Britannia* 23: 141–58
R. S. O. Tomlin (1996), 'The Vindolanda tablets', *Britannia* 27: 459–62
R. S. O. Tomlin (1998), 'Roman manuscripts from Carlisle: the ink-written texts', *Britannia* 29 (forthcoming)
S. D. Trow, 'By the northern shores of Ocean: some observations on acculturation process at the edge of the Roman world', in Blagg and Millett (ed. 1990): 103–18
G. R. Watson (1969), *The Roman Soldier*. London
G. R. Watson (1974), 'Documentation in the Roman Army', *ANRW* II.1: 493–507
P. R. C. Weaver (1972), *Familia Caesaris, a social study of the emperor's freedmen and slaves*. Cambridge
L. Wierschowski (1974), *Heer und Wirtschaft, das römische Heer als Wirtschaftfaktor*. Bonn
C. R. Whittaker (1989), *Les frontières de l'empire romain*. Paris
J.-P. Wild (1977), *Vindolanda II: the textiles*. Hexham
J.-P. Wild (1985), 'The clothing of Britannia, Gallia Belgica and Germania Inferior', *ANRW* II.12.3: 362–422
E. O. Wingo (1972), *Latin punctuation in the classical age*. The Hague
G. D. Woolf (1994), 'Power and the spread of writing in the west', in Bowman and Woolf (ed. 1994), 84–98

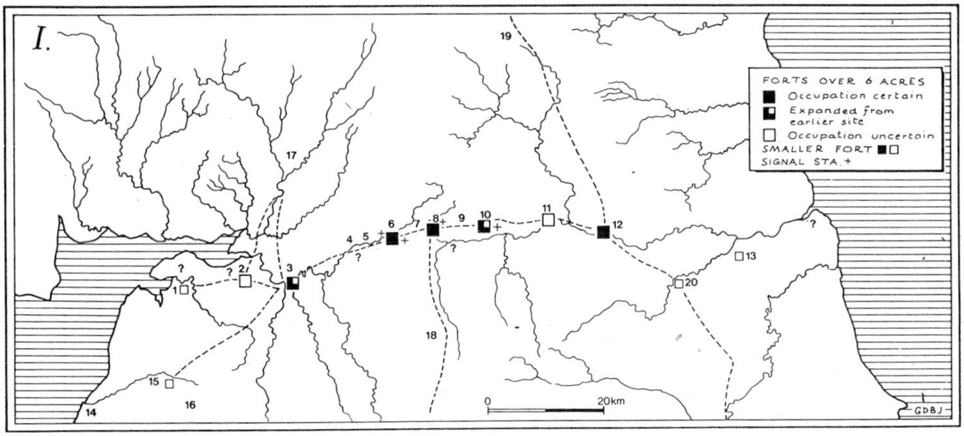

FIG. 1 The early Tyne/Solway Frontier I: *c.* AD 90+. 1 Kirkbride: 2 Burgh-by-Sands: 3 Carlisle: 4 Old Church Brampton: 5 Boothby: 6 Nether Denton: 7 Throp: 8 Carvoran: 9 Haltwhistle Burn: 10 Vindolanda: 11 ?Newbrough: 12 Corbridge: 13 Whickham: 14 Maryport: 15 Blennerhasset: 16 Caermote: 17 Broomholm: 18 Whitley Castle: 19 High Rochester: 20 Ebchester.

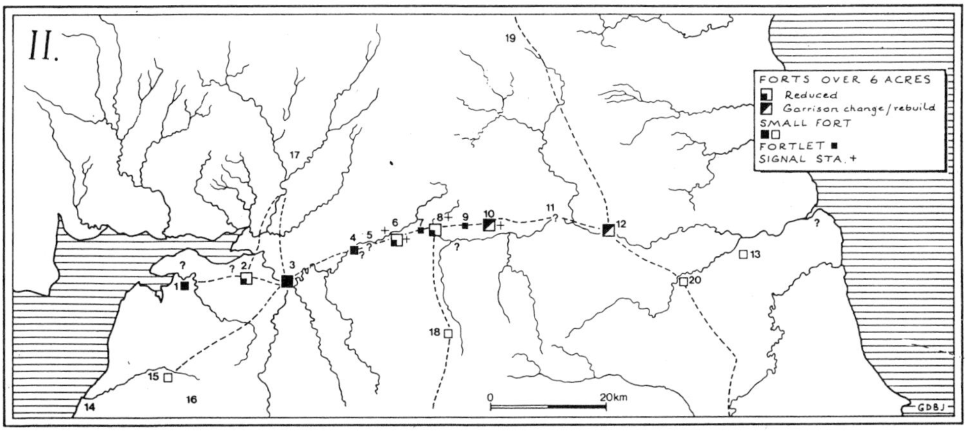

FIG. 2 The early Tyne/Solway Frontier II: *c.* AD 105+. 1 Kirkbride: 2 Burgh-by-Sands: 3 Carlisle: 4 Old Church Brampton: 5 Boothby: 6 Nether Denton: 7 Throp: 8 Carvoran: 9 Haltwhistle Burn: 10 Vindolanda: 11 ?Newbrough: 12 Corbridge: 13 Whickham: 14 Maryport: 15 Blennerhasset: 16 Caermote: 17 Broomholm: 18 Whitley Castle: 19 High Rochester: 20 Ebchester.

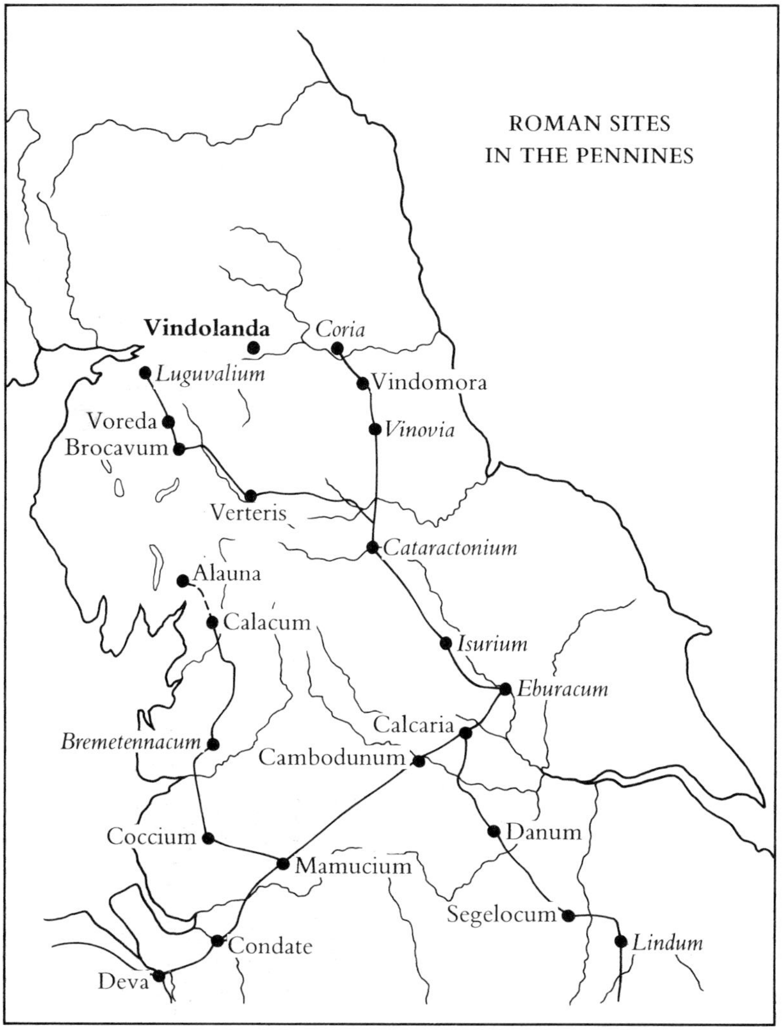

FIG. 3 The major Roman sites in the north of England. Only the principal roads are shown. Place-names which certainly or possibly occur in the texts from Vindolanda are in italic.

A woman's slipper from the Period 3 *praetorium* at Vindolanda, stamped with the maker's name, L. Aebutius Thales.

A textile sock from the Period 3 *praetorium* at Vindolanda.

A chamfron (frontlet of horse armour) from the Period 3 *praetorium* at Vindolanda.

Tab. Vindol. II 122. 90 × 36 mm. A fragment containing Latin shorthand. At the bottom right, upside down, there is part of a writing-exercise in capital letters.

Tab. Vindol. II 118. 100 × 15 mm. A line of Virgil's *Aeneid*.

Appendix, no. 1. 197 × 86 mm. Part of the strength report of the First Cohort of Tungrians.

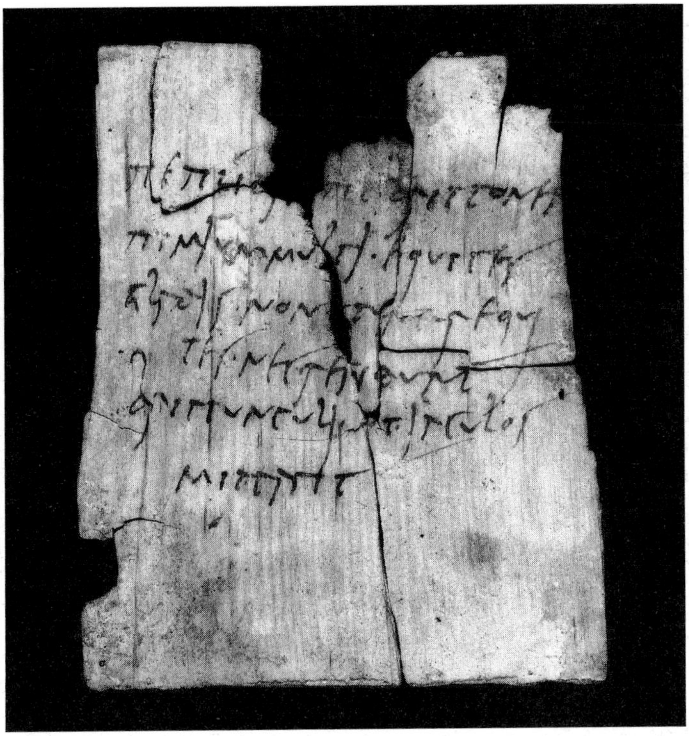

Appendix, no. 3. 78 × 186 mm. Memorandum about the Britons.

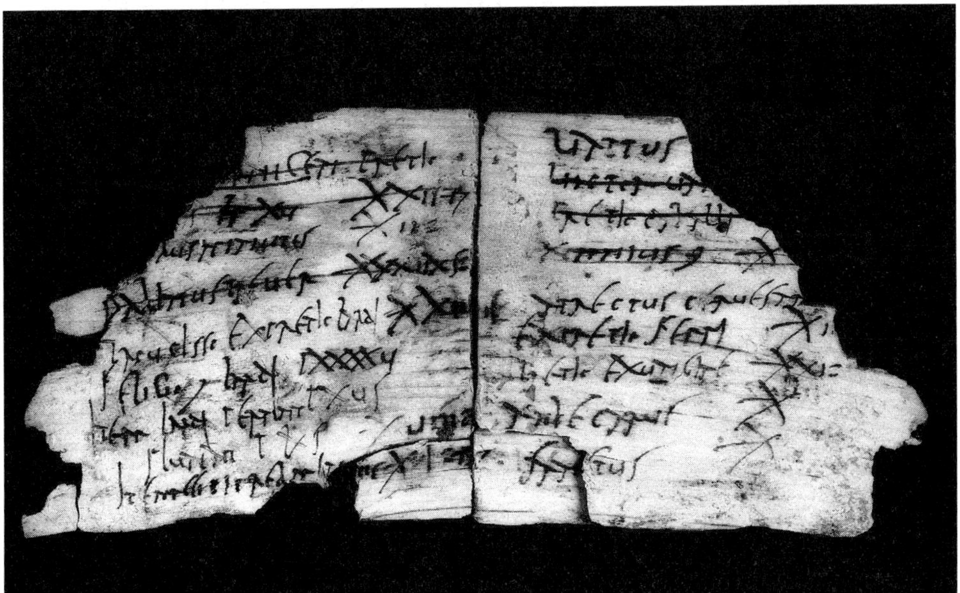

Appendix, no. 8. 174 × 77 mm. Account written in two columns.

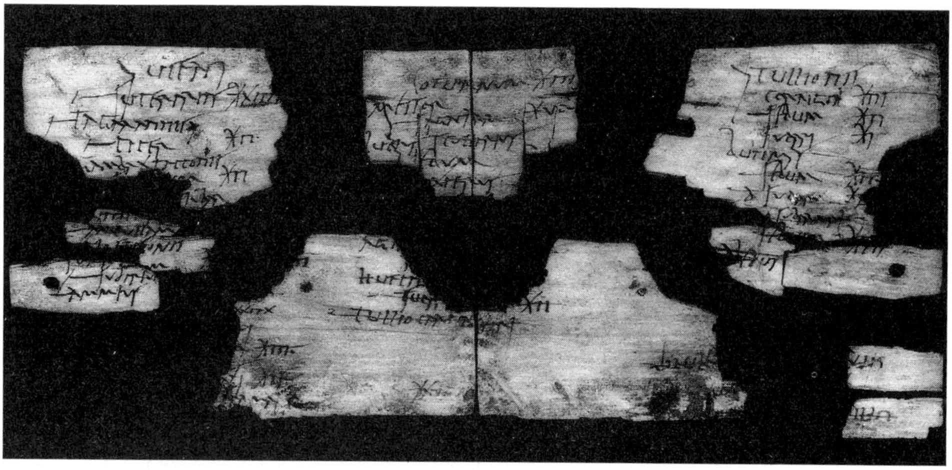

Appendix, no. 9. 210 × 70 mm. (approx.) Account written in three columns.

Appendix, no. 21. 223 × 96 mm. Birthday invitation from Claudia Severa to Sulpicia Lepidina.

Appendix, no. 28 (back). 99 × 70 mm. Address on the back of the letter from Chrauttius.

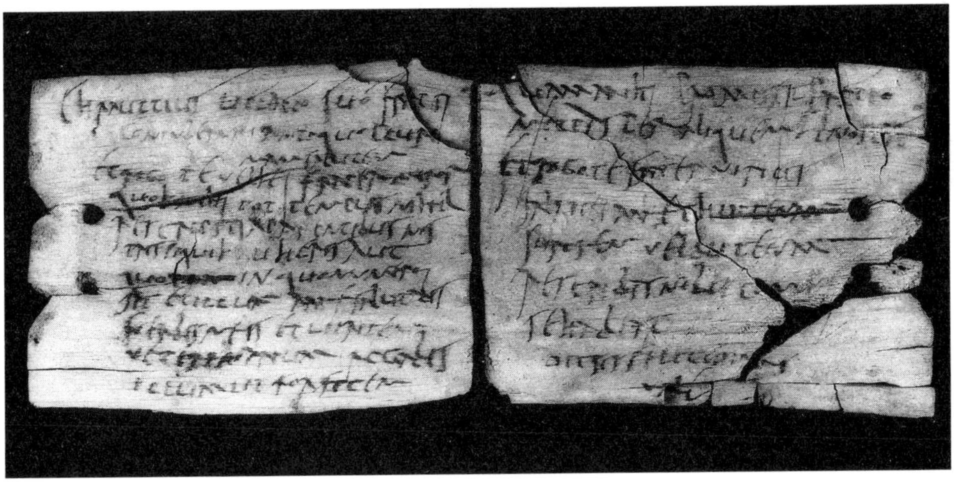

Appendix, no. 28. 189 × 70 mm. Letter from Chrauttius to Vel(de)deius.

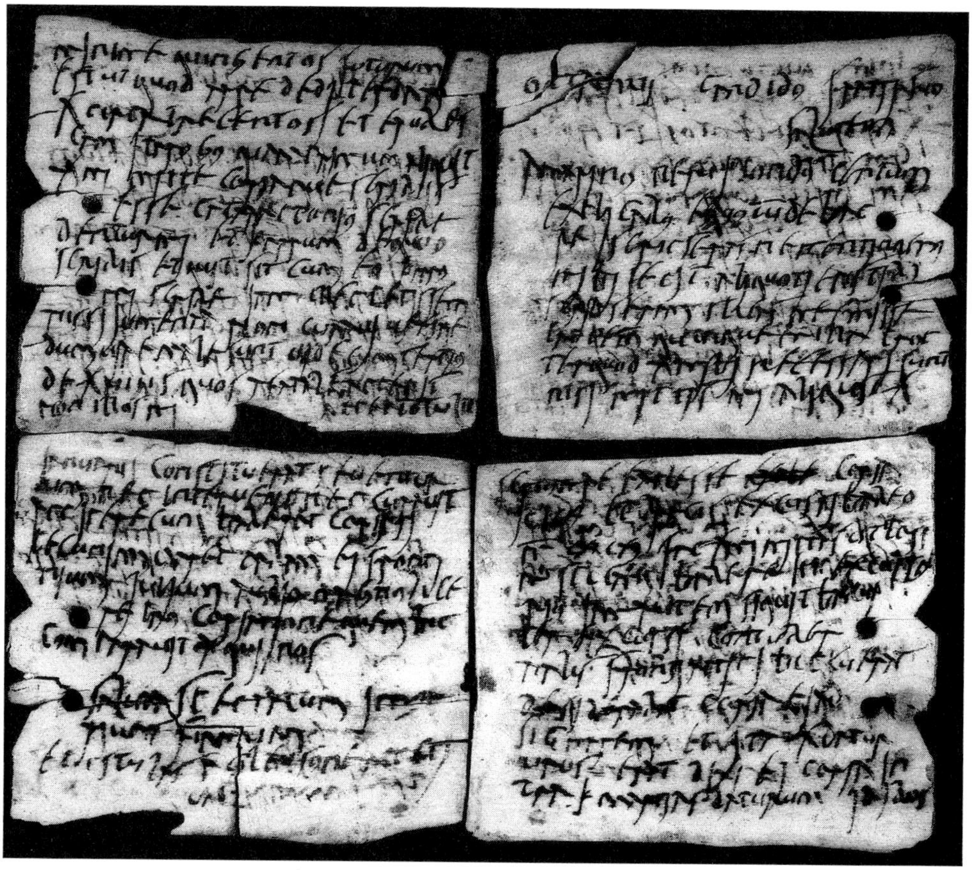

Appendix, no. 32. 182 × 79 mm. and 179 × 79 mm. Letter from Octavius to Candidus.

INDEX

ACKNOWLEDGMENTS

The author and publisher are grateful to the following
for permission to reproduce the illustrations:

FRONTISPIECE D. Woolliscroft
FIGS 1, 2, 3 G.D.B. Jones and K. Maude
PLATES I, II The Vindolanda Trust
PLATES III–VIII Trustees of the British Museum